THE ARCHERS

A Slice of My Life

A portrait of the author by Peter Rasmussen

THE ARCHERS
A Slice of My Life

Godfrey Baseley

SIDGWICK & JACKSON

LONDON

First published in U.K. by
Sidgwick & Jackson Ltd., 1971

ISBN 0 283 48495 5

Printed by The Whitefriars Press Ltd.,
Tonbridge, Kent
for Sidgwick & Jackson Limited
1 Tavistock Chambers, Bloomsbury Way
London WC1

CONTENTS

ILLUSTRATIONS

This book is dedicated to my wife Betty, in grateful recognition of her patience and help in adopting and accepting this very large family as a natural part of her life

PREFACE

IT WAS ON the first of January, nineteen hundred and fifty, that *The Archers*, an everyday story of countryfolk, began its extraordinary official existence.

No one at that time could possibly have forecast the impact it was to make as a permanent ingredient of sound broadcasting, and that at its peak, before the introduction of television, it would attract a regular audience of well over ten million listeners here in Great Britain. Never in my wildest hopes or dreams did I anticipate that it was to become, and continue to be, so much an integral part of my own life over all these years and that the characters in this imaginary village of Ambridge would become as real to me as my own family, friends and neighbours, and that I should get to know every field, wood, stream, lane, footpath and building better than I know those in the parish in which I live.

But that is how it is. Perhaps it is not so surprising, since nearly half my adult life has been concerned with collecting, researching and promoting the material that has gone to make up the programme and, even before that, the years of personal experience of living and working in a rural atmosphere and surroundings provided such a wide range of experiences, which all in their own way have played a part in laying down the right kind of foundations on which to build a structure that has proved to be so acceptable to so many people.

9

It would be very wrong of me to allow anyone to get the impression that *The Archers* is all my own work. It was certainly my own brain child but, like any other child, it has only grown up and come of age through the influence of a great many other people in all walks of life and through the expertise of the writers, producer and actors, whose belief in the programme is, and always has been, as great as my own.

In the following chapters I hope I shall be able to show just how the programme came into being and how the team works, and how through this team spirit, this phenomenal chronicle has become almost an essential ingredient in the lives of millions of people, not only in this country but in many other places in the English-speaking world.

I make no excuse in taking you back over the events in the early formative years of my life because I know quite positively that there have been, and still are, many occasions when the influences of events and experiences of those days find a place in the make-up of the programme.

I

Childhood

WHEN did *The Archers* really begin? This is a
question that has been asked many times. I
have pondered it on countless occasions
without finding anything like a positive answer. There
are plenty of milestones along the road of development
that would seem to be equally significant, but always one
remembers some previous event or circumstance that
played a part, perhaps a very minor part of the story, but
which nevertheless cannot be ignored. So now that I come
to set the whole story down on paper, I find the only safe
thing to do is to go right back to a date in October when
the present century was scarcely four years old.

That was the day I was born to Walter Ernest and
Mary Ellen Baseley in the Worcestershire village of
Alvechurch. I was just another male descendant from a
long line of Baseleys that stretched back for over five
hundred years, most of whom were farmers and countryfolk living in the neighbouring county of Warwickshire.
It was their blood that coursed through my veins, it was

their characteristics that I had inherited, dyed deep in the mysteries and experiences of life in rural England.

My father was the village butcher. That was the way he earned his living. But when the shutters were put up on the shop front and work was over for the day, then a completely different person emerged, in complete contrast to the accepted picture that one conjures up of a butcher of that time.

Father was the leading light in the village Shakespeare Society – secretary, producer, scene painter, stage manager and leading actor in the annual production staged in the tithe barn at the High House farm. He was so keen on Shakespeare that he would cycle the twenty-odd miles to Stratford-upon-Avon and stand in the queue for the gallery, probably for hours. Then at the end of the performance he would face the journey back home by the light of a flickering oil lamp on his bicycle.

Sir Frank Benson had a great influence on my father and one of the great moments in his life was when, at the invitation of Sir Frank, the Alvechurch Shakespeare Society gave a matinée performance of their current production at the old theatre at Stratford.

Father was an active member of the local Literary and Debating Society, the Choral Society and the Dickens Fellowship, and, after Adult School on Sunday mornings, as a knowledgeable naturalist he would take my sister and myself and our friends on long walks and gently initiate us into the ways of the wild creatures, the flowers, the trees and the history of the village and the surrounding countryside.

My mother also had an interest in these same activities, and in addition, in a simple way, through the playing of our American organ, gave me my first interest in music.

Mother shared in the work of the business and had quite a reputation as a pork pie maker. These pies were made on the kitchen table. It was early breakfast on pie-making days because they had to be finished in time to go into the village baker's oven after he had finished baking his bread. The baker's was two hundred yards away across the village square, and the finished pies were placed on a large baking sheet and carried on top of a head. There were some fearful moments on windy days. Mother was also a pioneer among lady motor cyclists.

Schooling for me in my early days was really a procession from one school to another, because I have to admit that I was a bit unruly and much more interested in any kind of boyish mischief than in any form of academics. One aspect of my very early life was, however, fairly constant. I had inherited some of my parents' ability in the world of histrionics, and in spite of all my misdoings I was prominent in the usual end-of-term concerts.

Having used up, as it were, all the available local schools, there was only one answer left – boarding school. My parents were members of the Society of Friends and they packed me off to what was then considered to be a daring experimental form of education at a co-educational school at Sibford, a village set in the heart of the Oxfordshire countryside.

Looking back over the years and comparing the way most schools operate today, it is difficult to conceive how the school was considered 'daring'. Certainly we had a good deal of freedom to go and do what we liked, and boys and girls mixed freely and were treated as equals. But make no mistake, the Headmaster, the late James Harrod, was a very strict disciplinarian who, in spite of the accepted pacifism associated with Quakerism, could, if necessity demanded it, wield a long-handled clothes brush and apply the back of it to the rear of offending pupils. I speak from experience.

I remember one incident very clearly. It was during the First World War. Father had sent me a 'pot' of apples (40 lbs) by train to Hook Norton Station, so on Saturday afternoon – a free period – I set off with a friend to walk to Hook Norton, three miles away, to fetch it. The walk there was easy enough – but the return journey for two twelve-year-olds struggling with 40 lbs of apples in a square wicker basket was very different. It was well after dark when we returned to the school. The trouble was that no one knew where we had gone – I didn't want anyone to know about the apples because I knew that I would not have been allowed to keep them for myself and my friends, they would have been shared out amongst everyone. That is what did happen, and the clothes brush came into action to teach me not to be selfish and greedy.

You won't find my name on the school's honours boards, but no doubt, tucked away in some dusty file, I have been recorded as an active participant in school plays and entertainments.

What the four years at Sibford did do for me was to develop, with the help and companionship of the staff, my interest and love of the countryside, and to help me to get to know many of the farmers, the tradesmen, craftsmen, and all the ordinary folk that the freedom allowed us to meet, talk to, and work with.

The experiment had worked with me. I was tamed sufficiently for my parents to consider sending me to Bootham, the Quaker public school at York, to put a bit of polish on me, to pass my matriculation examination and fit me up to join one of the Quaker firms in the

Midlands.

I didn't pass my 'matric'; I did just get my second eleven colours at football and cricket. I won a bronze medal for life saving at swimming. I seem to remember that I threw a cricket ball further than anyone else had ever done at the school sports. I was in all the drama productions, and an active member of the school Archaeology Society.

After four years in a mixed school at Sibford with a fairly free association with the girls, I found the rules and regulations of a boys' public school very restricting, but by diverse means, including climbing down a drainpipe from the bedroom at night, I managed to organize an assignation with a local schoolgirl in Bootham Bar. I have a strong suspicion that Arthur Rowntree, the then Headmaster, must have communicated the fact to my parents that my academic chances were slight. At any rate my stay at Bootham was cut short and I returned home to look for a job.

This happened just after the end of the First World War, and in the depression that followed there seemed little likelihood of my getting the kind of job my parents had hoped for.

Father was not the kind of man to see his son hanging and mooning about. He wanted some return on the sacrifice he had made and the money he had spent on my education. So a dozen times a day, or so it seems now, he would say to me, 'I've got a nice little job for you, get your bike out and take this little parcel,' or 'There's a truck-load of pig meal up at the station, get the horse and float and fetch it and stack it in the granary,' or 'There's some pens want cleaning out,' and so it went on day after day; and of course the inevitable

15

happened, my search for a job was over, I'd got one, working at home for the princely sum of ten shillings a week and my keep.

The job suited me well at that time. Delivering meat with a horse and cart all over the countryside brought me in contact with people in all walks of life, from the staff at the 'big houses', farmers, smallholders, tradesmen, to the most humble cottagers. I went to the markets to drive the cattle and sheep home along the country lanes. In fact, I soaked up the whole atmosphere of country life, including making the most of leisure pursuits.

I joined the Shakespeare Society and the Choral and Operatic Society in the next village, helped to organize socials, took part in concerts, danced at local 'hops', played chess, cricket and hockey. My interest in the theatre grew, I studied elocution and drama at the Birmingham and Midland Institute under Stuart Vindon and toured the country pot-hunting with some success at drama and musical festivals.

I took part in an experimental scheme to read poetry in pubs in Birmingham and took part in dozens of plays and sketches. One sketch that I particularly remember was called 'Buying a Gun'. With my friend, James Holliday, we performed this sketch all over the Midlands. In fact we did it so often that I got tired of saying the lines as written, but made them up as I went along. Poor Jim never knew what was coming next or where he was expected to pick up his cue.

I became an active member of the Birmingham Repertory Theatre Playgoers' Society, and occasionally played some small parts in the theatre's productions. I had a season at the Alexandra Theatre in Birmingham, I taught elocution at a Birmingham night school, but still most of my time was taken up with working at home. My interest in my job began to take second place to my other interests, but I was afraid to take the plunge and make the theatre my life, so I carried on.

Then came the advent of broadcasting and the permanent establishment of studios in Broad Street, Birmingham. Several of my friends had taken part in productions, so I applied for an audition. My application was accepted, and the day came for me to show my paces. Charles Brewer was the producer in charge.

I had no idea what to do at an audition, but as I had recently performed the part of Sir Toby Belch in *Twelfth Night*, I asked if I might do the whole of the drinking scene, playing all of the characters, including Maria. It must have been dreadful but, unbeknown to me, an actor who was to have played a part in a sketch that night had telephoned to say that he had a bad attack of laryngitis and couldn't speak.

The voice I used as Andrew Aguecheek must have sparked off an idea to Charles Brewer, and at the end of my ordeal he came into the studio and invited me to play the part in the sketch that evening. It was quite a small part – a country bumpkin.

I heard no more for months. Then the sketch was repeated, and I was invited to play the part again, which, of course, I accepted. Between rehearsals, Charles Brewer asked if I would try over some work that he provided – another audition in fact. This must have been all right because from that time I began to make regular broadcasts, sometimes as many as three a week, but I still dared not take the big decision to make this my career. So on I went, unhappy in my job at home, but quite prepared to accept it as inevitable.

The extra money I earned from broadcasting made it possible for me to get married to a farmer's daughter whose family tree stretched back as far as my own, but this time into the history of Worcestershire. We produced two daughters, Jane and Helen, and though we both hated the job I was in, this made us play for safety with a sure living. I'd tried unsuccessfully to get a job as County Organizer for the Young Farmers' Club, and one on the staff of the BBC in the farming section.

Broadcast engagements, however, increased. I was now taking part in drama, revue, musical comedy, Children's Hour, reading poetry and collaborating with a writer to provide material for documentary programmes.

The moment had come, and a few extenuating circumstances made us take the plunge. Very much to my father's disgust, I gave up my job and threw in my lot with broadcasting. To leave security for the unknown was a tough decision to make. But it worked. More and more contracts poured in. We were on top of the world and we spent the money freely in our home and on the children.

Then in 1939 came the war. All BBC contracts were cancelled and in a very short time our slender funds were exhausted. I went to work at our local Air Raid Precautions Centre for the princely sum of £3 a week, less deductions. Furnishings were shuffled round in the house in order to accommodate two teachers who were evacuated from Birmingham.

My talents for acting and producing proved useful to me in the Civil Defence. I was attached to the Police Sergeant in charge of the Report Centre to help organize exercises and demonstrations in collaboration with the other services and the Home Guard. It was all great fun and a valuable exercise in co-ordination and organization, an experience I have been glad to draw on many times since then, including work behind the scenes in *The Archers*.

But it was no use. With our growing family we simply could not exist on the money I was getting and what my wife was able to save out of the meagre allowance for our evacuees. So I got a job at a local aircraft factory, a soul-destroying, monotonous job in the time office. But by doing this we doubled our income.

There was another very welcome bonus at this time. The BBC had taken up residence in a country house near Evesham and programmes of a lighter nature were being produced, and out of the blue one day came a contract for me to take part in a programme called *Stairway to a Star* with Charles Maxwell as the producer. The fee for half a day's rehearsal and the live performance the same day was almost as much as I was getting in a week for my deadly dull job.

My boss knew I was unhappy, and shut his eyes to my absence for most of one day a week, when I would cycle to Evesham, nearly twenty miles away, and back again. The series had a long run, and the fact that I could produce a wide range of voices and dialects kept me in constant work.

Then came an event that was to change the whole course of my life.

Glancing through the *Birmingham Mail* one night, I saw a picture of a loudspeaker van that was being launched in the Midlands by the Ministry of Information, to tour around to stimulate recruiting for local defence and 'Dig for Victory'. There on the picture as the local representative of the Ministry of Information was a face

19

I recognized instantly. It was Denis Morris, who had been a Talks producer at the BBC in Birmingham before the outbreak of war.

I read the caption that accompanied the photograph to learn that this van was the first of a number to be launched. This looked like a wonderful job. If only! I was an actor, I'd done some writing. Wasn't it feasible that I could combine the two and become a speaker! I took a chance and wrote off right away offering my services.

I got the job. To begin with, I would have to accompany the two staff speakers already appointed, Louis Fenn from the Labour Party and Martin Gilkes from the Conservatives. It was planned that we should eventually work as a team dealing with the subject 'The war and YOU'. Louis and Martin were to outline the story of the war and I was to follow by indicating the way the audience could help in a positive way.

After a few days in the office to become acquainted with the set-up and to absorb some of the technique, I set off with Louis Fenn to a lunchtime meeting in the market place in Walsall.

On the way, Louis suggested that it might be a good idea if I dived in at the deep end as it were, and did the whole of the talk.

The loudspeakers blared out some martial music, the crowd gathered, and Louis introduced me to the assembled company. I knew what I had to say off by heart but with a great sea of faces in front of me I panicked, and in less than two minutes I dried up. I had simply and solely given the basic propaganda message.

Louis quietly took the microphone from my shaking hand and proceeded to give me the most important lesson

I had ever had in my life – and one that has stood me in good stead ever since. He took these hard unpalatable facts, one by one, and with all the skill of a top class politician, used them as a basis for a dramatic human emotional story that had its impact on every member of that vast crowd.

Little did I realize at the time that this technique was going to be repeated time and time again in *The Archers*.

I spent two years as a Staff Speaker for the Ministry, covering every sort of situation from assisting with vital communications after the disastrous air raid on Coventry, urging people to 'dig for victory', urging married women to take part-time work in factories, organizing tours for the pioneer commandos to meet workers at mass meetings at factories, to urge them to greater effort to 'provide the tools'.

At the Ministry I had almost arrived at the stage when I really believed my own propaganda exhortations. It was at this time that I reached another important milestone in my life.

About this time, the BBC were gradually returning to a situation of normality, and their studios in Birmingham were opened again. Denis Morris went back on to the staff as Head of Programmes with the responsibility to get things moving again.

After a few months, I enquired about the possibilities of a staff job. My name went on the list and shortly afterwards I was interviewed in London to assess my ability to become an Outside Broadcast Assistant. I was short-listed and was one of two people to be appointed on a temporary basis. I received notice of this and an offer of employment on the 17th April 1943. I was to start work on 1st May and my remuneration was to be at the rate of £650 a year, payable monthly in arrear.

How we celebrated this good fortune, and I'm sure we did, or how we existed for the month without pay, I don't remember. It had taken thirty-eight years of life and experience to qualify, but now the weight of all our worries, our anxieties and fears of the future were suddenly lifted – we were on top of the world. There were some horrible clauses attached to the contract; it seemed as if I was to be possessed body and soul by the Corporation. But who cared? I signed, and almost raced to the post box to catch the earliest collection.

That fortnight of waiting sped past. I learned with something of a shock that I was to take up my appointment in London, not Birmingham as I had hoped and imagined. I said goodbye to my colleagues at the Ministry, one of whom came to my aid by loaning me her tiny flatlet that she had retained while she was working in Birmingham.

All was ready, then almost at the last moment I was rushed into hospital with a suspected appendicitis. What on earth would happen? Would they fill the job and all our hopes be dashed? It was a nerve-racking time.

We needn't have worried, but at that time we didn't know how benevolent the BBC can be when occasion demands.

At last the day came. I said goodbye to the family and caught the train to London and the great unknown.

2

Early days of broadcasting

✳❀✳❀✳❀✳❀✳❀✳❀✳❀✳❀✳❀✳❀✳❀✳❀✳❀✳❀✳❀✳❀✳❀✳❀✳❀✳

THE Outside Broadcast Department of the BBC was housed in temporary quarters in Cavendish Square. I was to report to Frank Anderson, the Administrative Officer of the department.

My file was produced and I was enlightened on the working of the department and shown to an office that I was to share with two other new members of the department, Gilbert Harding and Frank MoreO'Ferrall, to await a meeting with the Head of the department, Michael Standing. After formal introductions and exchanges I tried to read and understand some of the papers that Frank Anderson had left for me. Although Gilbert and Frank did their best to make me welcome and part of the establishment I felt very much out of my depth – the country cousin in my utility suit against Frank's Savile Row outfit and Gilbert's distinctly individual style of clothes. The topics of conversation were at that time quite foreign to me; I was lost in a welter

23

of 'Outside Broadcast' jargon and sophisticated exchanges.

After what seemed an eternity the telephone on my desk started to ring. In great trepidation I lifted the receiver only to hear a charming female voice say, 'Mr Standing can see you now.'

This was the man whose voice was very familiar to me through his programme *Standing on the Street* where, day by day, he described the happenings in the streets of London and reflected the reaction of the people to current events. I certainly didn't expect to see this very young man towering nearly a foot above my head. I was very quickly put at ease as we talked about the wide range of interests that the Outside Broadcast Department had to cover, and Michael Standing skilfully interviewed me to discover how I should fit in and be used to advantage.

There was one piece of common ground that emerged very early in the interview. The members of the department had taken on and developed an allotment in Regent's Park and every week, assisted by 'Sandy' Hay, the man in charge of the Park, they did a live broadcast outlining the current work and the problems they, as very amateur gardeners, were facing. This was all part of the 'Dig for Victory' campaign – right up my street.

By the end of the interview, however, Michael had made it quite clear that I was not likely to take an active part in the programme until I had spent some time as an observer and had some closed circuit trials as a commentator and interviewer. These usually took place on the top of a high building where I had to paint a word picture of what I could see going on around me. These trials were recorded and played back – in company with

other play-backs of events that had actually been broadcast – at a full meeting of the staff. All very embarrassing,
but the critical comments made by Michael Standing,
Raymond Glendenning, his number two, and the rest of
the staff, which included Wynford Vaughan Thomas and
Stuart MacPherson, were exceedingly valuable and soon
I was able to take a more active part, first in *Radio
Allotment*, then in finding suitable people to be interviewed in the programme *Meet John Londoner*. Occasionally I did the interviewing on the air. I accompanied
Raymond to race meetings and football matches. I was
the chap who cut in saying 'square 4', 'square 2', etcetera
to allow listeners to know exactly where on the field the
action was taking place.

Within a month I was qualified as a full member of
the team. We were all interchangeable – with the exception of Raymond who was the star sports commentator
– and to gain extra experience I often took over jobs for
Gilbert and Frank, and the allotment became my special
responsibility.

After about three or four months of actively partici-
pating in and organizing programmes, an unexpected but
welcome opportunity presented itself. John Ellison, who
was the Outside Broadcast producer in Birmingham, was
making a name for himself in commentaries and programmes associated with the theatre, and the news must
have got through that a move to London might be good
for all concerned – whatever the reason, it was arranged
that we should change places.

The time I had spent in London had been most
valuable. I'd made many contacts both inside and outside
the BBC and I had acquired a good working knowledge
of broadcasting technique. What is more, my proba-

25

tionary period was over and I was now a permanent member of the staff.

There had – with the exception of the *Radio Allotment* programme – been no opportunities to present programmes of a rural character, and all the work I had done had been in a completely new field, reporting on topical events, sport, the world of theatre and entertainment, and all these had provided occasions to meet and work with experts in their own professions. I was going to miss all this, but the pull to get back to the Midlands where I was born and bred, and to be back home with my family, was stronger. So the changeover was made.

It took some little time to attune myself to the change from programmes and events of a national character to those that were essentially regional, although on occasions contributions were made to National programmes. As I have already stated, John Ellison had a special interest in the theatre and in my early days in Birmingham I continued and carried out the kind of programmes that he had established. Excerpts from Midland Theatre productions, variety from the Music Halls, *Works Wonders*, the *Army* and *Air Force Entertains*. These last two were programmes where one auditioned amateur artists ranging from aspiring grand opera singers to red-nosed comics, and built the result into a show. All good morale-boosting material. But the main part of my job was in organizing the events and making sure that all the relevant paper work was accurate and up to date to enable engineers and administrators to carry out their part of the operation smoothly and efficiently.

It was an intimate and friendly station and one knew

every single member of staff on Christian-name terms – except the boss, Percy Edgar. He remained 'Sir', but most lunch times he was to be found with Denis Morris around the snooker table in the club waiting for some opponents, and the 'pint' he often paid for after the game was the best of the day.

I was very happy in the job, and the long hours and travelling that were involved were no problem, but I often longed to get the smell of grease-paint and industrial smells out of my lungs and breathe some fresh air and meet more people from the world where I really belonged.

From time to time I went back to London to take part in some exercise that needed additional commentators or reporters and on one of these occasions I had the opportunity to put up the idea that we should pay a visit to a farm once a month and do a programme on similar lines to *Radio Allotment*, which had now come to an end.

The basic idea was that we should talk to the farmer and his wife and the workers on the farm to hear what they were doing and to comment on any seasonal activity going on *Down on the Farm*. The idea was accepted, and for the next twelve months Michael Standing, Raymond Glendenning, Gilbert Harding, Wynford Vaughan Thomas, John Ellison and myself became regular visitors to 'Longford's farm' on the outskirts of Stratford-upon-Avon. In wind and rain, snow and ice, and in sweltering heat we trudged round the fields, explored the buildings and gratefully accepted the hospitality of Mrs Longford as we satisfied our stimulated appetites with her farm-house fare.

These visits to 'Longford's farm' were a great success, and the size of the audience to my way of thinking

27

showed the interest the mass of the urban population had in the ordinary everyday lives of countryfolk. There was no thought in this programme of providing any information to farmers, it was pure nostalgia. Wynford's description of the muck heap emerged as pure poetry, Raymond brought excitement and suspense of his own brand to such ordinary things as milking and harvesting, and I leave you to imagine what Gilbert had to say about the mundane and seemingly simple and archaic operations.

Even in those days, which were long before Gilbert emerged as a national 'personality', he had on occasions a very sharp edge to his tongue, and I am sure that without really meaning it he could and did say some most hurtful things. He certainly upset my wife. I had gone with Gilbert to record a programme on 'guard dogs' that were being trained at Staverton near Gloucester, with me as the victim and Gilbert as the commentator.

The programme took longer than was expected and we were late returning to Bromsgrove where Gilbert was booked in to stay the night. We were still in the days of strict rationing and I knew that Gilbert would be too late for a meal at the hotel, so I rang my wife and asked her if she could possibly find something.

With great ingenuity Betty concocted a feast from our meagre supplies. Alas, nothing was right for Gilbert and it seemed as though he only ate the food under great sufferance – but the last straw came when Betty started to pour out the tea in our very best china. As was normal – and still is – the sugar and milk went into the cup first. Gilbert leapt to his feet and shouted, 'My good woman, don't you know that you should add the milk last?'

That is one thing you don't say to my wife. All her

'hackles' came up and she let him know in no uncertain terms that he was a guest in her house and who did he think he was to dictate to her. They had a real 'set to'. Next morning he was full of remorse and telephoned to apologize but I don't think my wife ever really forgave him.

Looking back, there was much in the happenings at 'Longford's farm' that we have rediscovered with Dan and Doris Archer, Walter Gabriel, Ned Larkin and the rest. But all this was still a long way off, though the powers that operate to shape our destiny could have begun to stir within me.

By this time the major crises of war were over. I had made my contribution by describing the way the Midlanders celebrated VE and VJ nights, and the events that occurred as members of the Forces returned home.

With these same Forces came the members of staff whose wartime activities had taken them to other engagements and occupations.

In Birmingham the structure of the BBC began to expand with specialist departments to cover music, drama, features, variety, news and recordings, and it was soon obvious that, unless I found some subject in which I could specialize, I should find that my section would cease to be creative in any way, and become a service section to provide outside broadcasting services as required by the other departments. I certainly did not want to become, nor indeed was I equipped to become, a desk-bound administrator. My very nature thrived on being out and about, meeting people, going places and doing some sort of creative work. What more natural than that I should try to fill the gap that existed in the new developing set-up and establish a greater understanding of all that goes on in the vast area of countryside within the Midland Region.

Without any conscious realization of what part the countryside was to play in the lives of millions of people in ten or twenty years' time, when the days of greater leisure arrived and people would be wanting to escape from the rush and hurly-burly of urban existence and find peace and relaxation in simple and natural pleasures, I felt the urge to get away from studios and all enclosed places and take the microphone out to the highways and byways, into the villages, to capture the pleasures and excitements of the traditional country sports and games. To meet craftsmen, naturalists, archaeologists, and just plain honest countryfolk and hear directly from them how their lives were spent at work and at play.

No doubt the influence of my early life at home and my schooldays in the quiet village of Sibford had become a part of me and, though by virtue of circumstance it had lain dormant, it was now re-emerging as a vital force.

I was allowed to experiment on a limited scale and from these experimental programmes evolved such programmes as *Sunday Out*, where three travellers, one on foot, one on a bicycle or horse and one in a car, explored a given area and came back to a high tea to report on where they had been, what they had seen and discovered. Sometimes they brought back with them some local person who had been able to contribute to their pleasure, to share it with us all.

We invited local people from each of the Midland counties in turn to come together and tell us what their county had to offer for those who liked to seek.

Another programme that emerged was *Country Calendar*, where countrymen and -women came to the studio to tell us of the wide variety of interests that could be discovered in the countryside as month followed month.

Quite apart from these county commitments, I was a keen follower of motor cycle sport. The BBC had covered racing, but never the growing interest in trials and scrambles.

The Midlands was the centre for the motor cycle industry and the BBC were being pressed to reflect other aspects besides racing. I was loaned a motor cycle and encouraged to take part in a trial and joined the Birmingham Motor Cycle Club. I thoroughly enjoyed myself and was so successful in one Boxing Day event that I qualified to take part in the 'British Experts' trial.

My next move was into scrambling and it was planned that I should do a commentary on what was at that time considered the top event at Nympsfield, near Stroud.

In order to make a better job of it and to be able to speak with some authority I entered for the first race on a lightweight BSA. It was three laps of the course, and on the previous day I had made myself very familiar with the difficult sections.

Then came the race. For two laps I led the field but about half way round the last lap I could hear someone catching me up so I decided to take a short cut – quite legitimate – over some very rough ground. Alas, I hit an ant hill and came over the top of the handlebars and dislocated my shoulder. There were no medical services on the course and I had to go on with the commentary on the big race, then rush back with the recordings to Birmingham before I could get my shoulder re-set.

All these programmes were in addition to the con-tinuing pattern of normal Outside Broadcast commit-

31

ments, covering church services, outside concerts, excerpts from theatres, variety shows and pantomimes. But gradually these were being absorbed into the departments where they rightly belonged, leaving me more time to specialize in my own field.

Then came a new – but welcome – responsibility. For many years, under the direction of John Green, a member of the London Talks Department, the BBC had provided a regular programme directed to farmers. This was planned on a national basis and designed to be of help to stimulate greater production to feed our people during the war and in the years that followed, and to keep farmers informed of the many new techniques that were emerging. There was a need for expansion, and for the programmes to have a more regional approach to help farmers within a more limited geographical area, and I was asked to be responsible for promoting this in the Midlands and working with John Green directly in this matter.

It was natural that we producers in the Regions should follow the established pattern that had proved itself over a long period of time, although we all had a certain amount of freedom in our choice of speakers to cover the main interests of farmers within our region.

Our normal choice – it certainly was so in my case – was to use scientists, research workers, lecturers from Agricultural Colleges and the more successful and outstanding farmers, and to leave the choice of subject matter to them to meet the requirements of time and season. It was great stuff. I myself was thrilled to be enlightened on the developments that were taking place,

May Day celebrations at Elvechurch Infants' School, 1910. The author is second from the right

Father, mother and sister Gwen. We pose for a photograph before setting off for a picnic. My early introduction to motor cycling

Learning the hard way. Trying to climb ' The Ladder ' at Nailsworth in Gloucestershire during a Birmingham motor cycle reliability trial

but rarely could I find an ordinary work-a-day farmer – the customer we were trying to get to – who was a regular listener. It seemed as though we were aiming at too high a target; those who could understand didn't listen because they knew already and the rest didn't listen because they couldn't understand, or even perhaps didn't want to change their methods and their ways.

At a meeting of all the agricultural producers I brought the matter up and asked if I could experiment on a magazine type of programme that would cater not only for the farmer but for his wife, his children and the farm worker. My theory was that the farmer's wife would have the programme on to hear the part that was aimed directly at her, and that her husband and the younger generation would automatically get their dose. As far as the farm workers were concerned I hoped that they would listen to matters that concerned them – and possibly bring up with the farmer points that they had heard in the more technical part of the programme.

It still didn't work – it was a bit better but the whole programme was 'bitty' and none of the sections could be given sufficient time to develop any subject. The situation was very similar with regard to the gardening programmes.

Then there was a change of Controllers in Midland Region. Percy Edgar had arrived at the age of retirement and John Dunkerly was appointed in his place.

Once he had settled in, and had a grasp of his job, he was anxious to meet the members of the programme staff to hear about their interests and the work of the various departments. He was no stranger to broadcasting in the

Midlands; he had been a producer himself for a time.

I was well down the list to be invited to tea in his office and a chat. But my turn came and the atmosphere was so informal and friendly that when the conversation got round to the subject of what was I doing and if I had any problems, I came right out with what was a real worry to me, that I had very few listeners to my farming programme, and that whatever I tried to do, it didn't improve the situation.

I'm sure that he thought that I was being over-pessimistic but he said, 'Would you like me to organize a representative meeting of farmers and others concerned with farming from all parts of the region and see what they think, and hear any suggestions they might put forward?'

This was terrific! Of course. This must be the answer, to sit round a table and analyse the situation and thrash out ways and means, not only of dealing with these subjects and matters that were of vital importance to the national economy, but to hear from such a group of experts and practical working farmers their views on how to attract the right kind of audience.

This promised to be a unique event in the history of broadcasting.

I went back to my office and began immediately to prepare a list of people who I considered would be valuable at such a get-together. I knew John Dunkerly would, for his part, be making contact with associations and organizations, inviting them to send a representative.

Time went by. I began to doubt the possibility of getting together, in one place, in one day, the people that we wanted and needed. My spirits drooped, as I plodded on with the old formula.

I had, in the meantime, persuaded Denis Morris, our lively Head of Programmes, to allocate me some time – five minutes around lunch time – to broadcast to farmers the daily state of the markets. This I felt would at least be a good way to make them acquire the habit of switching on the radio at a given time to hear the latest news of the rise and fall of prices, a matter of great and immediate importance to their pockets.

With the help of auctioneers from the principal Midlands livestock markets I was able to compile a good daily summary and to show the trends quite clearly. I also made the broadcast personally, rather than handing it over to a news reader. My reason for this was that from my past experience of attending markets, and my ability as an actor, I could present the report in language and terms farmers were used to and could understand. For instance, instead of saying such and such a grade or type of animal made up to thirty pounds ten shillings, I made it 'thirty pun ten'. It was a very big chore to know that every morning one had to face the kind of mathematical problems that such a programme produced and translate these hard facts into a script that was readable and easily understood.

I remember that my new secretary at that time, Norma Guise, who in a burst of enthusiasm had said she would undertake the job of preparing the figures and working out the average rise and fall shown at all the markets and for the Midlands as a whole, burnt a great deal of midnight oil and shed many tears.

But it worked, and gradually this programme began to be talked about among farmers when they met at markets and meetings.

At last the day came when I heard that the proposed meeting of farmers and others concerned with farming was fixed. The number accepting the invitation was so great there was no room big enough to hold it at the BBC, so it was to be held in the City of Birmingham's Council Chamber.

I was to attend of course, but, and this came as a great blow to me, I was to take no part in the discussion, just listen and absorb. I didn't understand this attitude at the time, but the 'powers that be' didn't want me to influence the meeting in any way. I'm sure this idea came from Denis Morris, who as my boss at the Ministry of Information knew that, through the experience I had had as a professional speaker and haranguer of crowds, I could possibly influence the meeting. It was flattering but very disappointing.

The Council Chamber was packed. Comments, criticism and suggestions came from all over, but, alas, practically all the ideas that followed were the old established ideas with a few variations. The meeting ground on and then from near the back of the chamber a big man, whom I recognised as Henry Burtt from Lincolnshire, stood up and said, 'I've listened very carefully to all that has been said and discussed, but it seems to me that what is really wanted is a farming *Dick Barton*.' And he sat down.

The whole meeting broke out into uproarious laughter – *Dick Barton* was the current horror and suspense daily serial, a 'soap opera' where every episode ended with an almost impossible cliff-hanger which forced one to listen the next day to find out how Dick, Snowy or Jock extricated themselves from a seemingly impossible situation – and when some sort of quiet prevailed, the Chairman brought the meeting to a close.

'A farming *Dick Barton*!' What a fantastic idea – but was it?

3

A 'farming Dick Barton'

W HEN all the guests had departed, those of us
from the BBC who were intimately concerned
tried to analyse and summarize all the many
points that had emerged at the meeting. There was no
doubt that our audience at least were anxious that the
BBC's policy of providing a programme directed at
farmers should continue. There were doubts about the
time of day the programme was broadcast, but the final
analysis showed the need for a service programme
directed to farmers on a regional basis. The 'Dick Barton'
reference continued to cause some amusement, but in the
end it was suggested that I should study the many points
that had been raised, and that I should have some further
discussion with Denis Morris as and when I was able to
formulate any new approach to the subject.

It was with very mixed feelings that I made my way
home. It was good to know that there was general
approval for the programme that I was producing but

it was disappointing that no new or revolutionary ideas emerged – that is if you ignored the 'farming *Dick Barton*' idea. But that was impossible.

All that night my mind was working on the problem and in the end I had to ask myself, 'Why should a sound, sensible and businesslike farmer like Henry Burtt come up with such an idea?'

I'd met Henry before, I'd seen his farming, much of it was highly specialized – producing seed for cereal and vegetable crops. Henry had contributed to the farming programme on this particular aspect of farming.

In the end I decided there was only one thing to do. I would ring him up in the morning and try to find out why he had come out with such a fantastic suggestion. This I did, and was more than ever surprised when he assured me that his suggestion had been made in all seriousness.

'Look,' he said, 'this is far too big a subject to expound on the telephone. Why don't you come over and see me and I'll try to explain and show you what I mean.'

I accepted his kind invitation and as soon as possible made my way to the farm at Dowsby, near Bourne in Lincolnshire.

We sat down in his very businesslike office and he began to expound on his type of farming. He was growing crops to produce a commodity whose value was measured in pounds per ounce rather than per hundredweight. The cost of producing such crops was very great as compared with normal farming practice. Every period of their growth, their harvesting and threshing called for special care and skill. It all had to be sifted, sorted and graded under very strict regulations – in fact it was, all in all, a very intricate procedure, involving high capital cost, with

a large staff and their families dependent on him. Every
night he went to bed knowing full well that at any time
wind, rain, drought, flood or fire could not only ruin him
but could be equally disastrous for all the people concerned with the enterprise – even to the farmers and
market gardeners who were depending on him for their
supply of seeds.

We left the office and went on a tour of the farm to
look at the crops and to learn how the land had to be
managed to produce the right kind of healthy crops. We
saw all the machinery – very costly machinery – that was
involved at all stages and the vast factory-like buildings
where the basic materials were stored and conditioned
before this 'gold dust' could be produced.

I remember one example very clearly. At that time
Henry was virtually the only producer of seed from which
'mustard and cress' is produced. He took me through the
whole chain of people who would be affected if by some
sudden stroke his crop should fail. It began with Henry
himself and his staff, then the growers whose glasshouses
would be empty, their staff, the makers of containers, the
transport people, the wholesale market men, the shopkeepers, the hoteliers and caterers and last but not least
the housewife and her family.

Oh yes, there were dramatic and highly emotional
possibilities in this, and I began to see what was in his
mind when he put forward his serious suggestion for a
'farming *Dick Barton*'.

But, dramatic as it all was, this was very much a
minority type of farming and bore little or no relationship
to 99·9 per cent of the pattern of British farming. Of
course the subject would make an exciting play for radio
or a film but it would be impossible to sustain such a topic

40

in a daily radio serial.

I went home fascinated but disappointed that I hadn't found the answer to my problem, but all I'd heard and seen, coupled with the idea of a daily programme to farmers, became very fixed in my mind. After all, I'd got a daily market report that by its very nature went some way towards compulsive listening, and there was the weekly programme addressed to the family as a whole that was useful but not compulsive.

Over the following months I tried desperately to find a formula that would incorporate the basic features of both programmes. There were lots of informal discussions with colleagues in other departments and with the Head of Programmes.

A great deal of time was spent trying to produce a format on paper, but all to no avail; it all ended up in my wastepaper basket.

It was infuriating to know that all the ingredients were at hand to make an interesting and informative programme if only a way could be found to blend them together in the right proportions to command attention.

While all this effort was going on, the regular programmes had to be produced. My time hadn't been entirely wasted because during this period of search and research, and studying the various ways that farmers gathered knowledge and information, it became apparent that the majority took their lead from what they saw being done by their neighbours. From this I devised a programme under the title of *Over the Neighbour's Hedge*. In this programme I went back to the technique that had been so successfully used on 'Longford's farm' but instead of using commentators who were well-known personalities, I chose a farmer who was very well

41

respected and known for his practical and successful work on his own farm. This was G. T. Williams from Newport in Shropshire, a very active member of the National Farmers' Union, who later became its National President. Each week G.T. went, with microphone in hand, to visit a farmer and talk to him about the way the particular farm was run, the crops he grew and why, the stock he kept and how it was managed. In the course of the conversations we learnt how progress had been made, and which methods had influenced that progress. G.T. was able to comment on what he saw and give his own reactions as a practical farmer.

This was all 'off the cuff' natural material emerging as between farmer and farmer, and what was most encouraging to all concerned was the definite increase in listeners, not only farmers but many townsfolk to whom it brought a breath of fresh air.

But alas, all good things have to come to an end and for a variety of reasons this was going to be the case with *Over the Neighbour's Hedge* and I was back again looking for something to take its place.

By this time, I had acquired a lot of 'know how' about farming through my close association with practical farmers, scientists and teachers. The same could be said about the techniques of radio production that I had obtained from my colleagues in the Drama and Feature Departments. Slowly the idea began to emerge of a studio production in which all the information I had to hand, or could easily acquire, could be used. Was it possible to create a character – a farmer – who could become a 'universal' neighbour? He would have a wife, a family, workmen on the farm and, as required, good and bad neighbours.

42

Out came the paper again and I scribbled away. I filled pages and pages. I had, of course, talked over the idea with Denis Morris and received some encouragement to press on and produce a script so that it could be properly assessed from all points of view. I had a vast amount of material at my command, I knew how to tackle the actual production of a radio play or feature, I knew the characters that were to speak the words and what they were to say. But when I put it down on paper it failed to come alive.

In sheer desperation I threw the lot in the wastepaper basket – and probably went out to have a pint or perhaps it was two or three or more to drown my sorrows and offset my feelings of frustration.

The following morning I regretted my action of casting all my work into the wastepaper basket, but alas it had been emptied by the cleaners and was on its way to the incinerator. Ah well, that was that! I sat down at my desk to deal with the work of the day and, lo and behold, there were my papers, straightened out and stacked in a neat pile in proper order. My secretary, Norma, who had shared the hopes and disappointments and had typed out my scribblings over and over again, had rescued it – just in case. I went through it again, all good stuff, but it was as dead as a dodo. How on earth could we breathe some life into it?

It had simply never occurred to me that what was wanted was the skill and craftsmanship of a professional writer. Anyhow the kind of budget that I worked on made no allowance for such extravagance; besides, all the writers I knew were as far away from farming as the North Pole is from the South. Still, having got this far surely there would be no harm in exploring the idea.

The nearest writer to hand was one who had been extremely successful in writing all kinds of material that had been broadcast from Midland Region, and over and above all that he was one of the current writers of, what do you think? *Dick Barton*! His name? Edward J. Mason.

I had actually been instrumental in starting Ted off on his career as a radio writer. We had a mutual friend, Mary Wheelock, who worked with Ted at Cadbury's. She gave me some material that Ted had written, lyrics and monologues. They were excellent but they were a copy of Stanley Holloway's style – Albert and the Lion and all that.

I asked Mary if her friend could produce some original material. Within forty-eight hours I was presented with a sheaf of paper with sketches and lyrics. This was good and I asked Ted to come over and see me. At that time I was only an actor working for the BBC but I was very friendly with Martyn C. Webster, the variety producer in the Midlands, and I felt certain that what Ted had written was exactly the kind of material that Martyn was looking for. I told Ted that if he could have patience I would find the psychological moment to hand it to Martyn.

It was several weeks before the chance came. I was giving Martyn a lift in my car from the studio to his flat in Edgbaston when he suddenly said, 'Damn, I've left a script in the office that I wanted to read, still never mind.' This was the moment I had been waiting for. I gave him Ted's work.

The next morning Martyn was on the phone to me the moment he arrived at his office. Who was the man who wrote this material? How could he get in touch with

44

him? I gave him Ted's address. The result was a stream of work in revue, musical comedy, Children's Hour and eventually *Dick Barton*.

4

The first edition of
'The Archers'

WITHIN a very short space of time Ted came in to see me, and we adjourned to the BBC Club to discuss the matter over a pint of beer. I went over my idea in a great deal of detail, describing the characters, the general situation in farming, and a list of events that I thought would provide first class material for creating highly dramatic and emotional situations.

I was delighted, when Ted eventually had a chance to get a word in, to hear him say that he would like to have a 'go' at it. So down to the office we went and I handed over my precious bundle of papers to him, and away he went.

My desk seemed very bare; for months it had been littered with books, leaflets, pamphlets and my own notes. But this was to be just a temporary lull, because in what seemed no time at all Ted was on the phone to say that he had been through the papers and was sure that something could be made of the idea. He wondered if he might

46

bring his co-writer of *Dick Barton*, Geoffrey Webb, in on the idea. Geoff was a countryman born and bred and Ted was confident that Geoff could play a very valuable part in the project.

'Yes, of course, if you think it is a good idea, the more the merrier,' I said, 'but you do realize, of course,' remembering my BBC training, 'that there is nothing certain about this, and I very much doubt if there could be any payment at this stage.'

'That's all right,' said Ted, 'we understand.'

So a meeting was arranged between the three of us after I had talked the matter over with Denis Morris.

We had our meeting and I was delighted to meet two such enthusiasts who were quite convinced that there would be no difficulty at all in creating a daily serial, not just a weekly episode, out of this subject. After all, a lot of spade work had been done. The family characters were real enough, so were those of their neighbours. There were plenty of situations that they said could be enlarged on. 'No problem, we'll let you have a sample script in no time.'

I was thrilled to bits that two such accomplished writers should be so enthusiastic and anxious to get on with the job right away. I was on top of the world.

What I did not know at that time was that the fabulous programme, *Dick Barton*, was under a bit of a cloud, not that it was losing ground with listeners, but because a rather noisy minority were accusing the BBC that through *Dick Barton* they were contributing greatly to the disturbing increase in the number of juvenile delinquents. Mason and Webb were slightly apprehensive about what attitude the BBC would take over this matter. They hoped that the programme would continue, of course, but all the same there would be no harm done in having something else on the go, just in case, and this farming idea might be just the kind of insurance that they needed.

It wasn't very long before the promised script arrived on my desk. It was immediately typed, properly laid out as a drama script should be. All very impressive. With high hopes I started to read it. At this distance in time I do not remember much of the detail, the number of scenes, how many of the characters were included or even what the theme of the episode was all about, but when I came to the end I knew that it had a gay beginning and an end that held you in suspense, but the middle was as foreign to the rest as a sugar-coated rhubarb pill. That waste-paper basket was very handy and very tempting, but fair do's, that was a first impression. I read it again and made notes, and then again, and although it bore little or no relationship to the successful *Over the Neighbour's Hedge* programme from which I hoped it would develop and carry the same degree of truth and sincerity, it did have some parts in it when voices came to my ears rather than the typed words to my eyes.

One thing was very certain – there would need to be a very close co-operation and method of co-ordination between the three of us if the project was to do all that was hoped for it.

It took many more meetings and much discussion before we arrived at exactly the right format and established the exact amount of education, information and entertainment that the programme could carry to keep a proper and acceptable balance. I was conscious of an air of optimism about, and this was sufficient to urge us on to greater effort to establish certain fundamental principles.

Firstly, the name of the programme. Was our working title right? We tried out all sorts of names that could be easily identified with farming, but any name that started with a consonant meant that either the announcer would have his lips closed or, as in the case of 'B' or 'G', would mean the emission of a thin sound. The boldest sound of all came from 'A'. I knew a family of Archers who farmed in the West Midlands and were fairly typical of the kind of farmer I wanted to represent. So we settled for *The Archers*.

Now for the type of farm. In order to cover a wide range of interests it had to be a mixed farm that was reasonably prosperous. Not too advanced in its method or technique but sound enough and just that little bit better than the majority.

We worked out its cropping and stocking, its labour and machinery requirements, working very closely to one or two farms that I knew quite well, including 'Summerhill', my wife's sister's husband's farm near Droitwich.

As it was going to be essential to refer to and illustrate the 'come day, go day' attitude of many small farmers at that period, we had to establish such a farm and farmer. We certainly could not let our central figure fall into this category. It was also essential that there should be a comedy element in the programme, not only to offset the educational aspect but as a source of entertainment comparable to the Music Hall comic.

This character – Walter Gabriel – had to be drawn very much larger than life. He had to be a fool to himself, but, however stupidly or wickedly he would behave, he must carry the listeners along with him and obtain their sympathy. This was a vital character because it was this type of farmer that the programme was fundamentally setting out to help. He was to represent the townsman's idea of the kind of 'character' farmer that you would meet in the village pub who could lay on the entertainment and take all the free beer that came his way.

He was to be the vehicle to carry the nostalgic elements, the recounter of old wives' tales, extraordinary cures for any ailment, a quoter of proverbs, a craftsman when he put his mind to the job. He had to appear to be an extrovert, but underneath it all was a sad, granny-reared creature whose wife had died and left him to rear their son, Nelson, who when we first met him would today be possibly classified as a juvenile delinquent – but who we saw as a slightly goofy moonstruck lonely adolescent.

To create a balance with the Gabriel set-up it was necessary to go to the other extreme and provide a farming situation that involved a rich industrialist who was ready to pour money into his new-found interest. This kind of character was needed so that we could reflect and comment on what was likely to happen through his influence on village life.

We were happy with the picture of rural life with the Archer family; happy that we had the necessary comedy material and its potential development. But there was another ingredient that Ted and Geoff knew from their writing experience was absolutely essential – Romance. What could be better than the sure-fire winner of 'poor boy meets rich girl'? So, to be ready for this situation, Grace Fairbrother was invented to become involved with young Philip Archer.

We explored all the possibilities that this basic pattern could provide in the way of human emotion, suspense, intrigue, tragedy, comedy and sheer nostalgia.

The fertile minds and expertise of Ted and Geoff gave me the confidence and assurance that all would be possible.

There were still a few minor, but at the same time vital, points to consider. First, the name of the Archers' farm. After a lot of discussion we settled for Wimberton Farm. It seemed to have a slightly West Country flavour about it. When, however, we came to listen to the announcer saying it, it was not bold enough – you have to draw your lips back to your teeth to say it and the vowel sound was thin. So after more discussion we felt that Brookfield sounded the right sort of name and, what was equally important, it was a universal name without any geographical association. A name that had the right ring was all important to the programme.

There was still one other matter that I considered to be vital to the overall pattern: the right signature tune.

It would have to be English, have a rural association without being over folksy. It wanted to be something that had a beat, immediately recognized and associated with the programme, one that did not get on your nerves through constant repetition. If it could be quickly learnt so that it would become part of any whistler's repertoire so much the better.

I went through dozens of records from the tunes of the day to Elgar, Vaughan Williams, Eric Coates, then at last I put 'Barwick Green' by Arthur Brown on the turntable. This was it. I played it again and again. Yes, this was it. I took the record home to play it over to my wife and get her reaction. It was immediate. Yes,

51

that's right! We kept playing it throughout the whole of the evening. The more we heard it the more we liked it. We found ourselves whistling it.

It is still there as fresh as ever after twenty-one years.

The decisions that were taken and the policy that was evolved have stayed virtually unaltered throughout the whole life of the programme, and in my opinion have been a valuable contributory factor to its success. At last we had got a sample script and a synopsis of what could follow but it was not 'home and dry' by a long way.

First I had to convince Denis Morris that it wasn't just a gimmick and that it might be worth while to give it a trial run. This was not too difficult because Denis, in his own time as a Talks Producer, had initiated a few revolutionary ideas, quite against the general policy of the department. But from his position as Head of Programmes there were many other angles that had to be taken into consideration, not least amongst them being the question of the budget which in those days was slender enough for the Region as a whole. To launch such a project was going to mean a very considerable increase in the amount of money allocated to my department, in fact such a project with five performances a week was likely to be as much as the existing cost of the Drama Department. Then there was availability of studios and staff to go with them and so on. But I did receive encouragement.

There was still another very big obstacle. How would the idea be received by my colleagues in the Agricultural department, particularly by John Green, the Head of the Department, who was normally academic in his approach to programmes? For several years I had been something of a rebel in my attitude towards the established pattern

of farming programmes, so it was with some trepidation
that at our next quarterly meeting I put forward the
idea. I did my best to prepare the way by quoting what
success, small though it may have been, I had had in
increasing the audiences by departing from accepted
policy – and then, hardly daring to pause for breath, I
hurled this latest bombshell into their midst. To my great
astonishment I was not shot down in flames or expelled
from the department. Perhaps they had by now got used
to my seemingly freakish or unorthodox ideas – but what
they did do, including the boss, was to laugh and jokingly
wish me luck and the rest of the business of the meeting
went on in its normal manner. I am sure that, at the
time, they considered me quite mad, but at a much later
date, when the programme was proving such a success,
they all went out of their way to offer congratulations.

But I go too fast. The signal is still at red. There is no
assurance yet that the programme will ever see the light
of day, but the time was not far off when Denis sent for
me to tell me that he was prepared to commission the
next four scripts.

We worked on these like mad and they were good, so
good in fact that we were allocated a place in the programme on the distinct understanding that this was to
be a trial run only.

How this decision came about I shall never know, but
I can only imagine that there was a surplus at the end of
the financial year and rather than return it to the general
fund it was decided to use it up. The mysteries of high
finance are quite beyond me, but the outcome of it all
was that we were allocated a quarter of an hour round
about eleven o'clock in the morning for five consecutive
days during Whit week, 1949.

With the signal now at 'go', selecting the actors to play the parts became a priority. There were plenty of good actors in the Midlands to choose from, and their work and ability was well known, so it looked like being a fairly easy job to make up the cast, but there was one problem. Although this trial programme was to be broadcast on the Midland Region wavelength only, hope of national coverage had to be kept very much in mind, so that meant that we had to be careful not to overdo any particular Midland dialect. So we set out to find actors who could interpret the character through the flexibility of their own voices – character voices, in fact, rather than a distinct dialect or an assumed Mummerset.

It was fortunate that there were actual scripts available for the auditions, and pains were taken to make the people who were up for the auditions fully aware of what was required.

At the end of the auditions, the cast list for the trial run ran as follows: —

Daniel Archer (the farmer)	*Harry Oakes*
Doris Archer (his wife)	*Nan Marriott-Watson*
Philip Archer (younger son)	*Norman Painting*
Christine Archer (daughter)	*Pamela Mant*
Jack Archer (elder son)	*Dennis Folwell*
Peggy Archer (his wife)	*June Spencer*

The first edition of 'The Archers'

Walter Gabriel   *Robert Maudesley*
(Dan's neighbour farmer)
Simon Cooper   *Eddie Robinson*
(Dan's farm worker)

Soon the first day of rehearsals arrived but before we all went into the studios we had a long session round a big table.

I was probably over-anxious but I knew that a lot of very important people would be listening with a critical ear and that the future of the programme depended to a very large degree on their assessment. I knew that none of the cast had any connection with the countryside or would be likely to know or understand what they were talking about in the play. So, rightly or wrongly, I felt that my first job was to brief each member thoroughly on the background of the character they were playing and also to explain very clearly the meaning of and reason for the action in the play itself.

This was a very tense moment for everyone concerned. None of the cast had ever taken part in a serial of this kind before, and for me it was the first time that I had produced a radio play of any kind although I had had a great deal of experience in handling other productions, but never one involving professional actors.

The fact that the production was to be broadcast live was no real worry to anyone; the days when there would be facilities for recording on tape were still a long way off.

The very first situation was one of anxiety about the birth of a calf. Dan Archer had to leave his farm worker, Simon, to look after the birth because he had to attend an important Farmers' Union meeting in Borchester.

The scene was set in the farmyard with Dan and Simon looking over the half-door of a loose box at the cow.

55

There was a low 'moo' from the cow, then Dan said, 'Well, Simon. What do you think?'

And Simon replied, 'Ah well – 'er might and 'er might not.'

In just those two lines we had laid the foundation of thousands of scenes and situations where anxiety, doubt and suspense have all played their part.

There was nothing special to remember about the week of rehearsals and performances. All cues were picked up on time, cows mooed, horses neighed and pigs grunted exactly as required. From our point of view, nothing more could have been done to make the show any better and as the closing announcement was made on Friday all we could do was to keep our fingers crossed and hope that the 'powers that be' were satisfied and that it had met the approval of the listeners.

As far as my memory serves me, it was a wet Whit week and most people were forced to stay at home and turned to their radio for their entertainment which, of course, included our offering.

The first real reaction to the programme came in the early part of the following week, when listeners began ringing up and writing to the BBC to discover what had happened to this new serial. They were getting interested and wanted some more.

There was no doubt about it, the exercise had been a great success and all of us who had been concerned with the project for such a long time were very anxious to get on with the job. But it was not to be for some time yet; in fact there were times when it seemed as though all was lost and the idea must sink into oblivion.

The reason for this was quite simple, though to the impatient and uninitiated very difficult to comprehend.

The regional budget could not be stretched to cover this new venture without making severe inroads into the output of other production departments which were already working on low budgets. Denis Morris did everything he could to try to persuade the Heads of the Home Service and the Light Programme in London to take up the serial. All to no avail. There must have been a great deal of lobbying going on at Broadcasting House in London that we knew nothing about, and I got to the stage when I had to accept the fact that it was 'a good idea while it lasted'.

Recordings had been made of the five episodes and these with copies of the scripts were still in circulation. Then towards the end of the summer it was announced that the Head of Light Programme was to retire and that Kenneth Adam had been appointed to the office. I have a strong suspicion, though I was quite unaware of the fact at the time, that some pretty powerful 'sales talk' was turned on to the incoming Head of Light Programme and I simply cannot accept the fact that it was just a coincidence that prominent in his 'In' tray when he first arrived in the office were copies of the Archers script and a note to say that recordings were available if required. However, the scripts were read, the recordings played, and all in good time the news percolated through that among some proposed changes that were to take place in the Light Programme, *The Archers* was to be given a trial run of thirteen weeks to begin in January 1950. The broadcasts would go out as before during the morning. The programme was to be produced in the studios of the Midland Region of the BBC.

Naturally those of us who had put so much effort and time into the project were delighted with the news, but we also realized that a lot of hard work lay ahead of us if we were to maintain the standard that we had set in the original trial.

5

Behind the scenes

T HE first big problem that I personally had to face
and overcome was how this new commitment was
to be fitted into an already full work and programme schedule.

As the Outside Broadcast producer, I was still concerned
in certain aspects with every broadcast that came from
locations outside the studios. I was personally responsible
for promoting and playing an active part in a great many
of these programmes. The daily market report was still
going out on five days a week. Every Sunday I produced
a farming magazine programme live in the studios in
Birmingham, then rushed off to a location that could be
anywhere in the Midlands to organize and take part in
the weekly gardening programme, also live. Then as soon
as that was over, during the twenty-six weeks of summer,
I was on my way again to meet the travellers in the
Sunday Out series and act as the link man in co-
ordinating their individual stories and shaping them into

a pattern that produced a good lively result. During the rest of the week there were such things as *Works Wonders, Workers' Playtime, Home Town Variety* and the monthly *Country Calendar.*

From time to time there were other commitments, like acting as commentator to cover big events that were of general regional or national interest.

It was quite obvious that with the responsibility of promoting and producing *The Archers* it would be impossible to deal efficiently with all this. The obvious first move was to transfer all programmes associated with the theatre over to the existing Drama and Variety Departments and this was followed by the majority of sports events. The reading of the daily market report to farmers was handed over to the announcer.

This left me farming, gardening and anything that was concerned with the countryside in general, and the occasional commenting where my own expertise and training was of value.

To deal with all the typing and extra paper work that would be involved with *The Archers*, additional secretarial help was supplied in the person of a very shy young lady, Miss Valerie Hodgetts, who for the first few months must have felt very bewildered in the hurly burly atmosphere of my office.

At that time it was difficult to conceive that this same young lady was eventually going to become such a vital part of the Archers team. But more of that later. Let us now take a look at that vital and critical period of planning the sixty-five scripts that would be needed for our thirteen weeks' run.

For my part, the whole object of the project was that the programme should be a source of accurate informa-

tion concerned with farming, not only on a seasonal basis
but wherever possible on a week by week or even a day
by day basis if any situation of a national character such
as, for instance, an outbreak of foot and mouth disease
demanded it.

From the writers' point of view the subject matter had
to have emotional potential that in turn would be associated with each of the characters or groups of characters.
It was also necessary from the writers' point of view that
strong emotional material could be offset or relieved with
comedy – suspense was also a vital ingredient.

Both Geoffrey Webb and Edward Mason had had a
long experience in the writing of 'soap opera' and other
forms of entertainment that they had created themselves
with no limits to their own vivid imagination, but, to the
best of my knowledge, this was the first time that either
of them had been asked to write scripts that came within
the category of the 'soap opera' technique but also had
to be accurate, feasible, probable and possible, and at all
times to keep the story topical.

Quite apart from the actual story itself, the characters
that moved about within that story framework had to be
so real that they were instantly recognizable and could
easily be compared with their living counterparts in every
village in the country.

I can assure you there were some very tough battles as
both sides or interests fought to establish their own
principles, and gain the respect and understanding that
eventually brought us to common ground.

There were a number of occasions during this period
and in the years that followed when we would talk and
argue for two or three days, often running into the night
as well, before we could agree on the manner in which a

particular story, once it was accepted that it was a story, should be woven into the fabric of the programme as a whole. We never actually came to blows, though it might have looked a likely possibility to anyone who could have observed us on these occasions.

Another interesting situation often arose during these 'story conferences'. Far from it always being a battle of wills between me and the writers, there were occasions when one or other of the writers would come over to my side in the argument against the odd one out, or I would move over to the support of one or other of the writers to convince the odd man out that we were right and he was wrong. Majority decisions were useless; they had to be completely and absolutely unanimous.

On many occasions during the period, and indeed throughout all the time Geoff was a member of the team, we would go through all the throes of creating a story or a sequence of stories and come to complete agreement. Then Geoff would go quiet. We would know that he was making a mental summary of all that had been said, then when he was ready, and it was usually brilliantly timed, he would rub his hand across his chin two or three times and very slowly say, 'Where's the torn drawers?'

What he wanted to imply was not that we should have included some violent scenes involving sex as a major motive, but that in the situations that had emerged we had omitted to relate or associate this basic human characteristic within the framework of our plans.

Another important policy issue that emerged during this period was that however valuable joint consultation and discussion was in settling fundamental matters, when it came to the actual writing of the scripts, the writer responsible for any given number of scripts should be quite free to follow his own personal dictates and judgement on the best way to interpret and develop the fundamental material. In the writing of a daily serial, speed is an important factor, and any kind of distraction, however well intended, is just not on. An episode that is written in fits and starts, or in which a flow of thought is broken, can easily upset the balance and will often show up in the actual broadcast.

It is important, however, in a serial like *The Archers* where authenticity is vital that a thorough check is made to make quite sure that the interpretation is quite accurate.

By the middle of December 1949 all was set. The first weeks' scripts had been duplicated, artists had received their contracts, publicity material had gone to *Radio Times* and all the arrangements had been completed with engineers, recording facilities were laid on, and so also were the staff to be responsible for effects.

By this time I almost knew the script by heart, and knew exactly what I wanted the finished episodes to sound like but, as I had learnt at our trial run during Whit week, in a radio production success or failure can depend on the skill of what we called in those days a 'panel operator'. This was a member of the technical staff, an engineer who was responsible for providing signals through green and red lights in the studio to the actors and those people operating background noises on gramophone records. Often the actors were distributed in two or three studios each with different acoustics to show the difference between scenes that were supposed to be either indoors or outdoors. Not only did the actors in these studios need to be accurately cued in by the light signals, but the microphone had to come alive at the psychological moment.

Many drama producers could and did operate their own control panel, but this kind of responsibility was too big for me and so a member of the engineering staff was allotted to the programme.

I had known this young man for many years, even before the war when I was working as an actor and he was either operating the spot effects or manipulating the huge banks of gramophone turntables where records were whipped on and off at incredible speed with split second timing and with such accuracy that the needle always seemed to drop on the right spot every time.

After the war, where this same young man served in the Air Force, he returned to Birmingham to carry on where he left off and to qualify for better things. During his years at the BBC he had accumulated a lot of knowledge of radio production by working closely with very able producers like Martyn C. Webster, Owen Reed, Robin Whitworth, Edward Livesey and many others, and it was a great relief to me to know that he was to take over the technical aspects of the production. The name of this young man is Tony Shryane, a name that was destined to become synonymous with the programme.

Although, on the face of it, Tony's job was purely technical, it was very necessary for him to know and understand what each scene was about, where it was supposed to be taking place, and the relationship between the characters and effects that were necessary, so that he could arrange for the right acoustics, where and when to start the fades from one scene to another, with often a few bars of music in between to indicate a change of time

Early days in broadcasting: interviewing miners at the coal-face of Snubston Colliery in Leicester-shire

A Trappist monk at Mountsorrel Priory breaks the rule of silence to tell the story of how he came to be awarded the Croix de Guerre during the war

With Audrey Russell and Wynford Vaughan Thomas after a week's tour of Midland
canals, during which they reported every evening on the happenings of the day

At Longford's Farm: our hosts, Mr and Mrs Longford

in the action of one scene and another, where to position effects like a door opening or shutting or the exact level – sound level, that is, say, of bird song, cows mooing or horses approaching, passing and fading away into the distance. These are just simple examples, but there were often occasions when several distinct effects had to be blended together in exactly the right proportion. So it was necessary for us to work very closely together, and for him to make a study of the script at the earliest opportunity so that at rehearsals and the actual recording of the episode he did not have to read the instructions typed into the script, but could 'feel' them just as much as the producer could for the overall picture and the actors for their own contribution.

Recordings at that time were made on to very large record blanks that could be played for the full fifteen minutes of the programme but it was necessary so far as the production was concerned that the same techniques were followed as in a live broadcast. One went through from beginning to end without a stop. If any mistake occurred it could not be rectified, it meant back to the beginning and start again.

Right from the start, Tony was enthusiastic about the programme. It was a real challenge to him as it was to all the rest of us, and by virtue of his knowledge and experience through all the technical aspects of radio production he was able to contribute towards the solving of problems outside his own specialized responsibility and to make suggestions that helped to smooth out the whole operation.

It was this enthusiasm, and his quick grasp of what the programme was all about, that led to a dramatic change in his life and in mine.

After *The Archers* had been running for about a month, and listening figures showed quite clearly that it was steadily becoming popular, a big decision was taken by the Head of Light Programme and the rest of the 'powers that be'. It was that the programme *Dick Barton* should come to an end and that *The Archers* should go into its place at a quarter to seven each evening, a key spot in the Light Programme.

As far as I was concerned, I was overjoyed that my 'baby' had made such wonderful progress. Although we were all full of hope, I doubt if any of us at that time had really expected the programme to run beyond the thirteen weeks that we had been allocated. Our plans, storywise, had been made for that period and now that we could look at the project with a whole year to cover, we virtually had to come back to square one and take a much broader view.

In addition to *The Archers*, my other responsibilities still continued. By a supreme effort and a lot of help from my colleagues I had managed to fit everything in, but it was a severe strain and one that I certainly could not bear indefinitely. Also it was quite obvious that, at the pace *The Archers* used up story material, I would have to spend far more time on research and to try to broaden the whole pattern of the programme to cover a wider range of country interests.

Denis Morris was well aware of the situation. There seemed a fairly easy solution. Hand the production over to the Drama Department.

I was very reluctant to do this as I felt it was vital that I should continue to be responsible for the authenticity of its content and the manner in which it was used.

Out of all the many discussions we found a solution. It

was, I think, an unprecedented action to take. It was that Tony should take up residence in my office and, working in close collaboration with me, take over the actual production of the programme in addition to what he was already doing as the technical assistant.

I knew that Tony would have dearly loved to have been transferred from the engineering establishment on to the programme staff. There were, however, complications about this, but by a gentleman's agreement – you could do those things at that time – this change was allowed to happen, provided that he could be available from time to time for other productions and that he would still remain within the category of 'engineer'.

The producer of a programme carries great responsibility. Quite apart from the technical aspects of the job, his whole demeanour can have a great influence on the cast and the technical assistants. If he is excitable or irritable, this seems to be transmitted to everyone concerned. Over the years, working on a repetitive pattern like a daily serial, there are bound to be occasions when someone or other will, possibly through nerves, raise the tension and get everyone else in the same state as themselves. It is in situations such as this that the producer must assert himself. He is probably furious, and would dearly like to get the 'big stick' out, but in nine times out of ten, this is the last thing he should do. He should try to remain calm and unperturbed, whatever his real feelings may be. Tony has the ability to appear calm and to restore the proceedings to normal.

There is an outstanding example of this.

We had planned to make a reference to the final score in a Test match and a space had been left in the evening's episode to mention the result and for Dan

Archer to make some comments on it.

It was a very close thing between England winning or losing and virtually not till the last ball could we be certain of the result. This was at 6.30 p.m. *The Archers* went out at 6.45 p.m.

Within five minutes of the end of the match, Ted had the script ready. It was very short, about two minutes, but for some inexplicable reason Harry Oakes could not get the lines over. The more he tried the worse he became and so did the other members of the cast until it seemed as though the whole idea would have to be abandoned.

By now, it was 6.45. We could hear the signature tune coming out from the Control room, the programme was on the air.

Tony left his place at the control panel, came into the studio and suggested that everyone should relax for a minute and then have one more try. He returned to his seat, pressed down the key to operate the loud speaker in the studio and said, 'When you are ready.' The scene was perfect and although there was only about one minute before it was due to be broadcast, the calmness that Tony had shown had been transmitted to the actors and all was well.

This kind of situation has been repeated many times over the years and always with the same result.

It was a bit of a squash with four of us in one tiny office, particularly as time went on with the duplication of filing cabinets, telephones and all the other impedimenta of an office. But it worked.

Our shy young Valerie worked almost exclusively for Tony on *The Archers*, not only in the office but in the studio as well. It was the beginning of an association that slowly grew into romance and finally marriage.

That was still a long way off, but it soon became evident that through her extraordinary memory she was to become a very valuable member of the team. If ever we were puzzled about anything that had happened in the past that it was necessary to know about for the sake of continuity, one quizzical look in Valerie's direction and out would come the answer – chapter and verse. In fact we all began to rely on Valerie and with any kind of problem that cropped up the immediate reaction was to say, 'Where's Valerie? She's bound to know.'

Our team was now complete, each with their own responsibilities. Yet, at the same time, this group made up from individualists, each with strong personalities, were able to work together with a single purpose.

That is the way it has been over all the years.

6

The team

𝕏𝕏𝕏𝕏𝕏𝕏𝕏𝕏𝕏𝕏𝕏𝕏𝕏𝕏𝕏𝕏𝕏𝕏𝕏𝕏𝕏𝕏

I HAVE laid emphasis on the fact that *The Archers* is essentially a team job, and now I would like to tell you how this team is made up and how it works.

It is comprised of the editor, the writers, the producer and his programme assistant, the actors and the technical staff. This team divides itself into two distinct sections. The editor and the writers in one section have the joint responsibility of creating and supplying the story, and the producer with his staff, through the actors, must bring the story to life in all its detail in the other.

Before I begin to show the detailed working of each section, it is useful to know the aim and object of *The Archers*. It is basically very simple. It is to entertain, to inform and to educate. It is to all intents and purposes a free interpretation of the BBC's own motto.

The most important ingredient in this mixture is entertainment. Information and education must take their place, but unobtrusively, even unconsciously.

The team

It is my firm belief that each one of us can be entertained in our own particular way. Some people need the stimulation of broad comedy to get their entertainment through hearty laughter, some are happy to find amusement from situations that have a similarity to those of their own experience. Others, as each new incident or event emerges, like to work out their own solution to the problem. Many more enjoy the opportunity to have a safe 'peep' through the keyhole.

There are a few who are sadistic enough to get their entertainment through observing the sufferings and downfall of others. But I am sure that the great majority are happy to be entertained by being transported for a short period each day into another world quite apart from their own mundane way of life.

Under the heading of 'information' I am convinced that there are very many people who can find pleasure and satisfaction from events within the programme that go a long way towards satisfying the insatiable appetite most of us have for news and gossip or towards the acquisition of knowledge that falls readily into the category of 'Well, I never knew that before!'

Even our third ingredient, education, can come within the entertainment bracket to a great many people who are looking for a painless method of acquiring knowledge, even if it's only to 'keep up with the Joneses'.

So you see, although it is our specific aim to inform and educate as well as to entertain, these sections can with skill be contained within the overall sugar coating.

But let me hasten to add that never on any occasion when we are planning on a long or short term basis do we get out the book of rules to make sure that all these factors will be duly considered or, having made our plans,

71

weigh up each of the three ingredients to ensure a perfect blend and balance. It all happens automatically.

It is only when one looks back over the years and tries to analyse the reasons for the success of the programme that one is conscious that all this has happened and that if it were totted up one would find that it has worked out at something like 60 per cent entertainment, 30 per cent information and 10 per cent education.

In my book, this is a pretty realistic assessment of what happens in real life.

Now let us get on with the way the team works. Naturally, I shall deal first with the team of which I am a part because I know this work best of all, and also because it is from the work of this team that *The Archers* has evolved.

As editor, it is my responsibility to provide the basic material from which the programme is built. This means that I must have a complete knowledge of what goes on in the rural areas of the country and how what goes on affects the people in all walks of life who live in the country.

This knowledge I can obtain in two ways: firstly as an observer of, or participant in, rural life and secondly through contacts who are specialists.

As no one person could possibly know it all I make use of both methods. A lifetime's experience of living and working in the country makes it easier for me to appreciate changes and movement, and the kind of impact these changes are making on the people and with what result. Over the years, by virtue of the actual work I have been engaged on in broadcasting, I have built up a list of valuable contacts who are experts in their own particular fields.

The team

It will, perhaps, be easier to understand the work of the editor if I use a particular example.

I know a local landowner who farms part of his estate himself and has the rest of the estate let out to five other farmers. This has been the tradition on this estate for generations but two of the tenants are getting on in years and are not really capable of maintaining their farms to a proper standard. Another tenant, a younger man, who because of shortage of working capital has always found it difficult to make a go of it, is badgering the landowner to put up some additional buildings so that this farmer can specialize. The two other tenants are progressive men but are hindered because they cannot expand or increase the area of land to farm.

Here, then, is a real situation involving six people all well within the confines of one parish.

Because I know the people concerned I am aware of each one's attitude of mind and I can make a good guess at the economic situation.

What do I find?

Firstly, the landlord's point of view. He is farming five hundred acres, and he has the staff, machinery and equipment to absorb at least another two hundred acres without any further capital expenditure. By so doing he could increase the gross profit margin.

The land farmed by the two older tenants would be ideal but there are two reasons why he cannot put the idea into practice. Firstly, on humanitarian grounds. The tenants have been in possession all their lives. They were, in fact, born there. To move them out might kill them, or at least hasten their end. Secondly, even if he was really tough, he would have to prove neglect and this is far from easy and the whole case would have to go to

73

arbitration.

In the case of the other farmer, our landowner has no guarantee that, if he put up specialized buildings, his tenant would be capable of increasing his income sufficiently to pay the additional rent that would be necessary to repay the cost of the building over a period of years.

The landlord also knows that the farmer who wants to specialize, and is not able to do so, will possibly try to find another farm that will suit him better, and if this is the case, the landlord could sell the very attractive house and divide the land between the two other farmers and satisfy them without any cost to himself. In fact it would mean money in the bank from the sale of the house that he could plough back into the estate.

Here then, is a real life situation, full of drama, bringing to the surface all kinds of emotional reaction: fear, frustration, hope, joy, sorrow, desperation, aggression. It could produce tragedy and even comedy. All the participants in this drama have had to go out of their way to learn how to establish and defend these rights.

A perfect 'Archers' ingredient, you'll say. 'All I have to do is transfer the situation to Ambridge and get on with it.'

Of course, that is exactly what I want to do. But, first, there are many questions that must be asked and the correct answers obtained.

I must know if this is an isolated case. The Country Landowners' Association will give me the answer to that, and that answer is, 'No, it is not an isolated case and we could supply you with dozens of actual examples and the way some landowners have been able to solve the problem.'

Right, I am on firm ground, but I must make sure that

if we do proceed we have all our legal facts and arguments right. I can get these from the legal department of the Land Agents' Association. We are safe in this matter.

Now I want to confirm from the Ministry of Agriculture that if the landowner adds an additional two hundred acres to his existing five hundred acres that he is farming himself, then he can manage this with the same staff, machinery and equipment and if so how much more economic would the enterprise be.

The Government Agricultural Land Service should know about this; after all they are closely concerned with arbitration procedure and facts like this emerge at arbitration courts. 'Yes, this is possible, but by how much? Very much depends on how this additional land is to be utilised. The National Agricultural Advisory Service could give you some examples.'

The first thing the NAAS wants to know is where the farm is situated because it would be a very different picture if, say, it was in Lincolnshire as against Devon or Northumberland. I get some examples relating to the West Midlands but even then there are differences according to the crops grown or stock kept. But there are positive examples of profitability.

So far I have checked and clarified the essential details of the landowner's case and point of view. Now I have to carry out exactly the same procedure, but from the other farmer's side of the fence. First to the National Farmers' Union at national and local level. What have they been able to do to help and advise members in similar predicaments? Through the NFU I could easily be put in personal touch with farmers who have been through this kind of crisis in their lives and I would be able to get a personal story of all they did to win – or lose.

Through all these enquiries I have been able to clarify such matters as compensation for fertilizer residues, penalties for dilapidations, the cost of new buildings, the value of attractive farmhouse property, co-operation, bulk buying, but above all this I have become aware of all the intimate and emotional feelings and reactions of five real people, each with their own personal problems.

Over a period of years an accumulation of knowledge through dealing with such matters short circuits much of this routine enquiry but from year to year legislation can have been introduced that has altered some of the situations, so the story must be checked.

I have outlined one particular situation that could be reflected in *The Archers* but this same process must be followed for every event, whatever the subject matter may be.

The kidnapping of Adam, the hold-up at the Post Office, the mail van robbery, the shooting of a poacher and the case of Doris being accidentally knocked downstairs by an intruder and the manner in which she obtained compensation, were all thoroughly researched in collaboration with the police, with the points of view of both sides very much in the forefront.

To open a Field Study Centre in the programme we must know in detail how a real centre operates. It is the same with running a pub, the Post Office, an antique shop, a market garden, fruit growing, fishing, shooting, hunting, running a riding school, local government, education, anything at all that is part of country life. I could go on and on.

But let us go back to the story that I have outlined in more detail, that of the landowner and his tenants. I have got all the facts, and now the whole situation has to be looked at in relationship to Ambridge and *The Archers*. I am convinced that this is a good slice-of-life story that would provide the writers with a splendid opportunity to use their skill and powers of invention and construction, but have we got the necessary established characters to do it full justice? At this point the answer is no. Could we plan for this to have a place in the future and in the meantime introduce the necessary characters into the programme and allot sufficient time to get them well established, and their problems known and understood? This would mean at least five new characters but we could not ignore the woman's angle, or the impact on the families. Would the budget stand it? If it was given the place and priority in the programme that it needed, it would of necessity mean that we would have to hear less of the established characters. Would listeners mind – would they protest?

All this is far too big a decision to be made by one member of the team, so the matter goes on to the agenda for the next meeting of editor and writers. If I feel it is necessary, so that everyone is in the picture, to provide the writers in advance with the basic ideas and relevant facts, I do so. On the other hand, I may want to use an element of surprise, or it is possible that in a sketchy outline I may not have been able to get the full impact of the idea over to them and they have preconceived even a negative attitude to the matter. If so I wait for the meeting itself to outline the story and deal with each aspect as it arises. One thing is quite certain, the story cannot be imposed on them. We must all be in agreement or anyone opposed to the subject would not be able to produce a convincing script.

The story that I have outlined was put forward and discussed at one of our meetings. Everyone agreed that it provided plenty of good emotional material, but it just would not fit into the existing framework of *The Archers*, and if we had to take the proper amount of time to construct a framework, many of the problems would no longer exist. However, we bandied the story about, trying to find parts of it that we could use right away without much change to the overall pattern of the programme.

The final result bore no recognition to the original idea, but a great many of the most telling of the human problems did emerge.

You don't believe it? Then have a think back to what happened to Brigadier Winstanley's estate when he handed it over to Isobel.

What I have just told you is just one part of the editor's responsibility to examine any project in detail, but what I find most satisfying and exciting is planning ahead, and discovering experiments taking place and research being carried out that could possibly make revolutionary changes in the way of life, not only for the countryfolk but for the population as a whole.

I like to think of planning in three stages. At least five years ahead, a year ahead, and three to six months.

The long term planning means keeping a watchful eye on what is going on in the field of research with genetics, nutrition and biology, in advanced techniques concerning automation and mechanization, in pest, disease and weed control, keeping in touch with committees and commissions appointed to make a study of some particular aspect of country life. It means being aware of ideas and plans for the future of existing organizations like the Countryside Commission, the Naturalists' Trust, the Forestry

Commission, and other associations with a special interest in rural affairs.

At the same time it is necessary to become acquainted with extension work in trials and experiments of a more practical nature and to get a first-hand picture of what leading farmers are doing, and what they are planning to do.

Farming is closely geared to providing food for the nation, and to an increasing degree the High Street is having an influence on what and how these requirements are made available to the housewife.

Planning five years ahead may seem a long time. It isn't. It could take all of that time to change over from one pattern of farming to another, particularly if livestock was involved. In many instances, particularly in the world of genetics, ten years would be considered a short time.

The next planning stage is about a year ahead when one can be fairly positive that changes that have been observed during the long term are coming closer to becoming accepted, or are likely to be having an impact on the people.

At this stage it is time to make the writers aware of anything that is likely to affect the people of Ambridge and provide them with the opportunity to meet the people in real life who are closely concerned. They could be Heads of departments of various Ministries, scientists, engineers, executive officers attached to Boards, Commissions and Associations. But perhaps it is best of all to arrange visits by the writers to farms and other locations to get first-hand knowledge and the opportunity to see some action, and from what they see or hear to form some ideas on how it can all fit into *The Archers*.

The third stage is usually thirteen weeks ahead when

plans must be quite positive, because what is done at this stage affects the whole organization, and in the next chapter I'll tell you just how.

John Ellison tries to interview one of the hens

June Ball was the land girl on the farm

I interview Jack Tropman, the carter, behind his
horse-drawn seed-drill

Denis Morris, who made it all possible

Geoffrey Webb and Edward J. Mason, the original script writers, out on location

Tony Shryane, producer of *The Archers*, at the
control panel during an *Archers* recording session

John Keir Cross

7

How it's all planned

ONCE in each quarter of the year there is a Joint Meeting between the people concerned with the policy and planning of the output of Radio 4, the Head of Network Production and his assistant as the people locally responsible for administering the programme, the producer who, in addition to the actual studio production, is responsible for the day to day administration, the writers and the editor and a member of the BBC's Information Department.

The object of this meeting is to have a free exchange of comments on all aspects of the programme during the past thirteen weeks and to discuss its future. This means that the hierarchy are made aware of the content and development of the programme from the story point of view and that the producer, editor and writers can be made aware of any changes in policy that are likely to have any impact on the programme as a part of the whole output of Radio 4.

81

As an example, throughout its long run *The Archers* has, whenever suitable, reflected current news and events, but with the increase of news coverage and commentary on the background to the news in the overall pattern of Radio 4 it was considered and jointly agreed to reduce the amount of coverage in *The Archers* to items that were of specific interest to countryfolk and to consider *The Archers* more in terms of providing a distinct contrast within the overall framework and to provide a break and opportunity for listeners to relax from the kind of concentration required to take in the more factual material.

The day starts with the editor and the writers discussing and coming to an agreement about the story content during the coming thirteen weeks and beyond, which has been under discussion at previous meetings and location visits.

The stories will be arranged in their final order, and we shall determine the amount of prominence they will receive, the period of time they will need to run, and which characters will be involved in the kind of situations the writers will create.

When all this is completed we are joined by Tony Shryane, the producer, and our plans and ideas are outlined to him so that he is well in the picture and will be able to make his plans, particularly those concerning administration, well ahead.

He will be concerned with the forward booking of the actors who will have major roles to play. He will need to know the full background and requirements of any new characters so that he can either arrange for auditions or be able to select the right person to play the part from his own knowledge of the ability of specific actors. He will need to know of special recordings needed to create background atmosphere that are not already available in the library. He may well need to make recommendations for adjustment in order that the whole operation can proceed smoothly within the confines of the budget. If by any chance there are any plans in the story to include topical items to fit in with such events as the Royal Show, the announcement of the results of the annual Agricultural Price Review, or the Budget, he will need to make sure well in advance that all facilities are laid on both on location and back in the studios where they will actually have to be fitted into the programme, probably recorded as much as a month previously.

Then we meet the 'hierarchy' to outline our proposals. In most cases these are accepted without any kind of modification. There are also times when they are able to see greater potential to a particular story than we have seen ourselves. On the other hand, it could happen that there is some part of our story that could clash with plans already made, or future changes in policy would mean that we would have to look for a new approach in dealing with one of the problem stories that we had planned.

Generally speaking, there has been very little to alter or modify throughout all the years, although the representatives at the top have changed half a dozen times, and we are now working with our third Head of Programmes in the Midlands.

If I have made this quarterly meeting sound like a dull formal affair, let me hasten to correct the impression. It is an occasion when frank speaking is accepted as normal but much of the discussion will spark off personal anecdotes and references that are highly amusing.

From time to time, in our story plans for the future, we want to introduce some item that will provide a shock or seem quite revolutionary. The death of Grace Archer, Philip's first wife, was a case in point. We knew that it would come as a great shock to our listeners. It was unheard of at that time for one of the leading and most popular characters in a daily serial to be killed off. But from the writers' point of view such an event offered unlimited scope for a number of dramatic and highly emotional scenes which, after all, are the life blood of any serial of this nature. Dare we do it? The immediate reaction of the meeting was – why? It was then necessary to explain the reasons for this unprecedented step. We knew the reasons would have to be good and logical if the idea was to get full approval and backing. One of the big risks we had to take was that we should so upset our listeners that they would not continue to listen.

So what was it all about?

We had followed Grace and Phil from the first day they met. We had seen their friendship develop into love. We observed them through all the stages – often highly romantic stages – to the day they became engaged. We shared all their desires, their temptations, and were very much with them in spirit through situations when they were on the verge of submission to a pre-marital sexual relationship.

Everyone was happy at their marriage and wished them well on their honeymoon.

On their return we followed the whole pattern of two young people in love settling down to their life together and sharing their pleasures and disappointments. Eventually as was inevitable we had to come to a decision on whether they should start a family. If they did, then it was equally inevitable that they would settle down to a pattern of life that in most respects would be similar to other married couples in the programme and their impact would be lost. We did not want this to happen. After all Philip was destined for a prominent place in the future.

Then the idea occurred to us. What about letting Grace die and then we should be left with a young widower, having to face up to life and reality?

We had never had this kind of situation before and we saw endless possibilities before us right through to the time when Philip would marry again. This was a set of situations that appealed to us very much, but now came the problem of how Grace was to die. We didn't want to go through a period of illness and sadness. Whatever we did would have to be an accident and immediate. But what kind of an accident? We explored every possibility until we hit on having her sacrifice her life in a courageous attempt to rescue her horses from a burning stable.

That was the sequence of events that we presented and those were the reasons for wanting this highly dramatic event to happen.

To our great relief the situation was accepted but there was some doubt about the wisdom of actually having Grace die among the flames, after she had released the horses. After further discussion with exchanges from all sides of the table it was decided to reduce the horror by getting her out of the fire, but to let her die in the arms of her husband in the ambulance on the way to the hospital, a very strong climax to the story.

This, then, was the decision of the whole meeting and, having made the decision, we had to try and anticipate the results of our decision on our listeners.

As I have mentioned earlier, at this meeting there was a representative from the Information Department and he was quick to see that this event, quite apart from its shock value in the programme, would obviously get a big reaction from the Press and he was most anxious that news of our intentions should not leak out before it all happened on the air.

Here was a big problem. The programme was being recorded a fortnight before transmission date and this meant that a whole chain of people were involved, from the typist who cut the stencils from which the scripts are duplicated, right through to the actors concerned.

Furthermore, the scripts were normally in the hands of the actors several days before recording. What would be the effect on the performance of those intimately connected with the recording? The only solution to this particular problem was to temporarily change, for one week only, the recording schedule. The episodes containing the build-up on the actual event would be recorded on the actual day of transmission and as late in the day as possible. Furthermore, to reduce the risk, the actual scripts would not be duplicated or delivered to the actors until the very last minute.

This, then, was the plan to which every member of that meeting made his or her contribution.

Having gone so far, I must continue. From the Information Office a note went out to the Press. In addition to those concerned with radio reporting it was issued as a general release, inviting one and all to be present during the late afternoon of D day to hear the recording of a very unusual event.

Such an invitation obviously aroused their curiosity and this was heightened as they followed the episode on the previous evening.

At the time appointed, we had a very big gathering of

the Press. They listened in silence but as the closing music was faded in there was pandemonium. Interviews with the actors, the writers, anyone in fact who might have any sort of a story to tell. Then, suddenly, they had gone. They had rushed away to get their own story ready for the presses that within a few hours would start to print the next day's papers.

All telephone lines to the BBC were blocked by listeners for hours.

Those of us who had been intimately concerned in this most unusual episode made our way home to lose ourselves for a day or two until the turmoil could quieten down, but when the newspapers came out the following morning with frontpage stories with impressive headlines on almost every national paper, and most of them congratulated the BBC for this bold stroke, we were able to relax.

I think every paper in the country carried the story and I remember that the Salvation Army's *War Cry* took up the whole of their front page with the story, praising the programme for its bold yet realistic acknowledgment that death must be faced by everyone, even if it comes in the prime of life.

On this very same day another event took place. The first commercial television programme was transmitted, but even this auspicious event was completely overshadowed by *The Archers* in Press coverage.

Of course we were accused of choosing this particular date to stage our event, but I must leave you to judge for yourselves because you know now that our plans were made more than three months ahead.

The death of any character involves a lot of hard thinking. If the programme is to retain its value as an authentic story even the best loved may have to go at the appropriate time to make way for the next generation.

There is a limit to the number of times that an older character can be sent quite naturally away from the village. We could be in a position where an actor may want to give up, or be forced into such a decision by his or her own personal health, and we must carefully introduce some symptom to be associated with the character that will help to create the right sort of climate.

There is on occasion the need to kill off a character in order to create a completely new set of situations that could not occur if they were alive. The death of the Brigadier is a perfect example. We could then make a new appraisal of hunting within the framework of the programme. It brought the house and estate on to the market, thereby opening up a number of stories concerning 'human emotion' as we follow the fate of the tenants under a new landlord. It brought a change of mood and attitude towards the sporting facilities. It gave us a splendid opportunity to follow the restoration and furnishing of the house from a woman's point of view.

Although there would be no problems as far as the actor was concerned – I played the part of the Brigadier myself – it was important that the senior members of staff who were concerned with the output of sound radio, and Radio 4 in particular, should have the opportunity to consider our proposal and give it their blessing before we took any action.

As I have previously stated, *The Archers* is a 'team' job and the death of Grace is a typical example of just how that team works.

8

'The Archers' and television

✤✤✤✤✤✤✤✤✤✤✤✤✤✤✤✤✤✤✤✤✤✤✤✤✤✤✤✤

LONG before the death of Grace, the whole machinery of *The Archers* had settled down to a fairly routine pattern. Tony was still operating from my office and, owing to changes and developments in the other side of my work, it became necessary for him to take over a greater share of responsibility for *The Archers*.

Although we were able to discuss all matters concerning the programme by virtue of the fact that we were working in the same office, it was very rarely that I put in an appearance in the studios, and because of this I was able to give much more of my time to doing research and working with the writers. We went out on location a great deal, to meet real live farmers and to make contact with all the various seasonal farming operations. We were certainly not afraid of getting a bit of mud on our boots. But farming was not our only concern because, as time went on, it was brought very forcibly home to us that one cannot isolate farming from all the other activities that go on in a village. It was necessary to widen our horizon and explore the possibilities of forestry, market gardening, the world of local craftsmen and tradesmen. The whole social life had to be taken into account, the church, the pub, the village shop, the school.

From the very beginning we were determined to be accurate in all the farming facts that naturally emerged because you will remember that the whole reason for the programme in the first place was to provide, within its framework, a schedule for keeping farmers in touch with new and successful techniques. Brookfield Farm, with Dan Archer in control, was to be the universal neighbour. We went to great pains to make sure that all farming matters were completely true and accurate.

What we did not realize when we began to include other village interests in the programme was that our listeners would automatically expect the same level of accuracy and authenticity. Fortunately my own personal background over the years and past experience in the kind of work I had done during my time at the BBC were invaluable.

All this began to put an increasing strain on the writers because it must be remembered that in virtually all their previous work, particularly with *Dick Barton*, they could sit down to their typewriters with blank sheets of paper in front of them, bring their vivid imaginations into play and create any situation that they desired, however fantastic it might seem, without any challenge as to its authenticity or even its possibility.

It was very different with *The Archers*. They could still conjure up exciting lines of story development but now they had to be constantly aware that it carried sufficient truth and accuracy to be at least a possibility. It was not enough to rely on credulity.

For quite a while we had worked very much 'off the cuff', keeping our minds on the immediate problem and those that would be dealt with the following week, but as the horizon began to increase it was realized that if we were going to get anywhere at all it was necessary for us to look much further ahead, so that the facts relating to the subject that seemed to be necessary to the programme could be obtained and absorbed before the writers actually created the situation or story.

So I decided that at least once in each quarter I should plan a two-day trip out into the country to meet farmers and see and hear what they were doing, to go to research institutes and experimental farms. It was also important that the writers should become acquainted with the way farmers and their families amused and enjoyed themselves.

Wherever we went everyone was most helpful and enthusiastic to help us, and our interests ranged over Women's Institutes, Young Farmers' Clubs, Agricultural Shows, and Ploughing Matches, where we had a wonderful time getting close to the soil and absorbing the whole social atmosphere of the countryside.

One of the most important ploughing matches is held at Cruckton, near Shrewsbury. We had spent several hours watching the work and having all the various techniques and tricks explained to us; then at the end of the day we were invited by the farmer whose land had been used for the match to go back to his house and join a few friends, an invitation we gladly accepted.

I do not remember exactly how it came about but during the evening we were challenged to take part in a

91

most unusual contest, to see who amongst the assembled
company could eat the most raw eggs. What we did not
know was that the company included the local champion.

Trays of eggs were brought in, sherry and Worcester
sauce produced, and off we went. Ted was the first to
pack up at six, I went on to fourteen but by then the
sherry that I was taking with them was having more
effect than the eggs. The local champion went out at
somewhere round twenty leaving Geoff the winner. But
he didn't stop at that, he went on to make it twenty-four,
and he was taking his in gin. I am sure he could have
gone on, but at this point the supply of eggs ran out.

By working very closely with the writers I had begun
to understand and appreciate what kind of material they
required and, to a very large degree, how their minds
worked. I knew that it was no use suggesting anything
that did not provide an opportunity to capitalize on any
of the human emotions, or that could provide some
comedy.

This was the beginning of the editor/writer relationship that has proved so valuable over the years. It also
meant that I could work much more on my own and
that they had more time to concentrate on the business
of writing. By this time Tony Shryane was ready to carry
the full responsibility for the actual production of *The
Archers*.

Destiny was at work again. I had become the 'country
correspondent' of *Television Newsreel* in addition to my
other commitments and most weeks I was off on some
sort of assignment to cover news items relating to the
countryside.

It was a completely new venture for me to translate
a story from sound to vision. I was very fortunate to have

some good tutors. Phillip Dorte was the Head of *Television Newsreel*, Richard Cawston was one of the producers, Paul Fox and Michael Bulkwell were the script writers, and Edward Haliday – a royal portrait painter – was the completely unflappable news commentator.

Television was developing rapidly and there was a growing need for some programmes of a rural nature to be injected into the service as a whole. The idea was slow to materialize, but when it did I was offered the appointment.

This was a most difficult decision to make. It would mean uprooting my family, with the attendant problem of schools and 'O' and 'A' level examinations which were imminent. I was very happy working in Birmingham and my job was interesting and rewarding. How would I get on in London and what would happen about *The Archers*? Fortunately I did not have to make a quick decision and there was time to evaluate the full complications of the change.

There is an old proverb which says, 'He who goes not forward, stays behind,' and this epitomized the pattern of my life so far. By virtue of my very nature I simply had to accept the offer – after all it was a promotion, and these were early days of television and who could tell where this kind of experience could lead to?

The decision was taken. The family would remain in Worcestershire until the children had finished their schooling and I should go into digs until such time as we could set up house somewhere in the London area. To my great joy I was to continue as editor of *The Archers*, as it was thought that it would be some time before I should be involved in many television programmes.

93

My appointment as Rural Programme Organizer, Television, was confirmed but I remained on at Birmingham for some time until a successor was appointed. In the meantime, my secretary, Norma Guise, went on ahead of me into television to learn the ropes.

Apart from my friends in *Television Newsreel*, I was very lost among a lot of strangers and in trying to understand all the complexities of television, but fortunately I had had a little experience while working with Barrie Edgar in Birmingham in producing a country magazine programme from a farm near Meriden. It was in this series that Percy Thrower made his first television appearance when he commented on the seasonal work in the farm garden. So with a fair amount of bluff and persuasion I did get a television gardening programme going, with David Attenborough producing and Percy Thrower and myself going through the motions, many of them in garden settings that had been built on the roof at Lime Grove studios.

Once this gardening programme was established, I turned my attention to finding other outlets. Children's programmes started to include country material and so did the afternoon women's programmes. But by far the biggest impact came from the Outside Broadcast Department who developed the idea that had started in Birmingham of a farm visit and every Sunday during the summer months we were able to show what was going on *Down on the Farm*.

There were some tremendous enthusiasts in the Outside Broadcast Department at that time and between us we built and presented a most fantastic, spectacular programme from the Smithfield Show at Earls Court.

The value of the animals and the machines that took

their place in that programme ran into the millions – we had on show the top ranking bulls and cows of virtually every breed in the country. It was the same with the horses, the sheep and the pigs, to say nothing of the very latest in farm machinery.

After two years' working in television, country programmes had been established as a natural part of programme output. Midland Region had taken over the responsibility for farming and gardening and the West of England at Bristol became the centre for programmes covering the whole range of natural history and country pursuits. David Attenborough had played a very big part in opening the door through the success of his *Zoo Quest* series.

Anyway my job came to an end. There was nothing else that I could move on to that satisfied me and obviously the BBC couldn't keep my small unit in being on the off-chance that something might turn up. I was offered a job, with an increase in salary, but I would have been desk-bound in a small office where telephone conversations had to be broken off every two minutes while a train rattled by.

I said goodbye to television, London and to the BBC as a member of the staff.

I look back on those two years with mixed feelings. It was very exciting to be part of a rapidly growing service and to know that I had been instrumental in introducing some new ideas that were going to become an established part of television, but in many ways those years were difficult and frustrating in trying to convince people whose life was mixed up in a world surrounded with bricks and mortar, whose major interests were closely bound to economics, politics, science, music, poetry and

95

all the rest of the arts, that there was another world outside. A world where the pace was steadier, where one could observe all the wonders of nature, a world that more and more people were turning towards to escape from the turmoil and complexities of life that they themselves were often helping to ferment.

After two years away from my family it was great to be back. Perhaps a younger generation was better equipped to bear the growing pains of this new medium in our lives. It is certainly a great responsibility to have even a minor part to play in steering the course of one of the greatest marvels of our age.

Although I had now left the permanent staff of the BBC I was re-engaged on a contract basis to, as my contract said, 'undertake editorial responsibility for the serial programme entitled "The Archers" which shall include your personal supervision and checking of all scripts before the programmes are recorded and your advice on agriculture and all other matters (whether topical or otherwise) relevant to "The Archers" and any other duties reasonably required of you in your capacity as Editorial Consultant to "The Archers".'

This, then, was to be my 'bread and butter' as I started on another phase in my life, that of a freelance.

Over the years I had accumulated a great deal of knowledge about agriculture and knew how to use this knowledge to form a basis of a story. I was on very friendly terms with a vast number of people associated with farming and knew of their specific interests and problems. As a member of the Guild of Agricultural Journalists, I knew most of the leading writers on the subject. Surely there must be some way of making use of all this to provide me with additional income.

David Turner   Bruno Milna

Brian Hayles

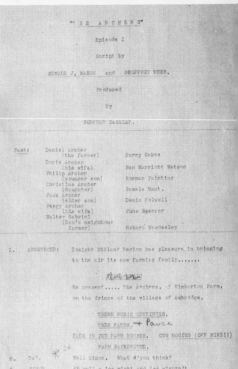

The front page of *War Cry* was typical of national press coverage after the death of Grace Archer

The first page of the first script of *The Archers*

An example of how organizations of international repute are prepared to issue bonafide documents to substantiate their belief in the programme

It seemed to me that I was well equipped to enter the field of Public Relations. In the course of my job I had met scores of men and women who had courted me in the hope that their clients' interests could be reflected in the programme. Their 'hand-out' material was as familiar to me as the daily papers. Surely this was the answer, to set up as a Public Relations Consultant. This I did, with some considerable success, but my first love was always *The Archers* and as time went on, and the requirements of the programme became more demanding, priority had to be given to the backroom work of *The Archers*, and slowly I let my interests in Public Relations fade out, hoping that I should be able to find some other form of outlet that would more easily fit into my new way of life.

This I found in writing – as the gardening correspondent to the *Birmingham Mail* and with contributions to a wide range of magazines in the form of editorials, profiles and special features.

The extra time that had to be spent on *The Archers* was a result of the changes that have taken place in life in the villages and rural areas. They were not dramatic changes that happened overnight and I doubt if many people living in the country had noticed the fact. But after living and working in London for two years, and now being a member of a rural community, I could see a very big change and it was obvious that life in Ambridge was not quite in step with reality. In my own village, new people with an urban background had come to take up residence and houses and cottages had been transformed into 'desirable residences'. The newcomers were taking an active part in village life. The old adage that one had to live in a village for forty years before one was accepted was proving to be a myth.

There were other changes. Men who had worked all their lives on the farms had been tempted away to earn far more money in industry and there was a much greater feeling of independence. The children seemed suddenly – to me, that is – to be better dressed and more intelligent. There were far more cars about and the village was no longer a tight, self-contained community but seemed as though it was slowly becoming a part of the nearby market town.

When I was able to look still closer at what was happening on the farms and market gardens, I knew that the picture that we were portraying in *The Archers* was not the picture of reality that had always been our aim. I am sure that the cosy nostalgic atmosphere that we were creating was very acceptable to the mass of our listeners in the urban areas, but those who knew the real situation could hardly refrain from a quiet chuckle whenever the subject of *The Archers* came up in conversation.

This situation simply had to be changed. We had somehow 'lost' a couple of years. It was obvious that we could not make the change overnight. To bring us back into step it would be necessary for us to introduce some new characters, not only to bring the population pattern into perspective but to be so involved that their impact on life in the village would be felt to the full.

There was still another important factor that had to be considered. Up to this time most of our attention had been focused on the village of Ambridge and the people who lived and worked in the village, but now it was necessary to broaden our canvas to include the parish as a whole, and to be able to get a glimpse of Borchester and Hollerton in the background.

It was, of course, with many regrets that we had to be prepared to lose certain aspects of the programme and there were doubts about how the new look would react on our listeners.

Then came a very big blow to the programme. Geoffrey Webb, who had been a tower of strength in the writing team, died. Ted and Geoff had worked together for years and could almost read each other's thoughts. I, too, through our close collaboration, had learnt to know them intimately, both as individuals and as a team, and although we were both aware of Geoff's failing health, his death came as a great shock.

What was to be the future? Could anyone possibly replace Geoff? It all seemed very unlikely, but like it has always been in the world of Show Business, of which I suppose we were a part, the Show had to go on. A new partner for the team had to be found who was capable of absorbing the whole atmosphere and technique from scratch.

9

The writers

✖✖✖✖✖✖✖✖✖✖✖✖✖✖✖✖✖✖✖✖✖✖✖✖✖✖

GEOFFREY WEBB was a big man. He stood over six feet high and tipped the scales round the sixteen stone mark. He liked big cars, and a big house with plenty of room to move around in, both inside and outside. He had a big appetite and adored unusual and exotic food. He had a thirst to match. He worked big and played big. But above all this he thought big.

This particular aptitude was of immeasurable value in the formative years of *The Archers*. It was never enough for Geoff to take a particular incident, however simple and seemingly commonplace, and deal with its immediate impact. He would want to explore and exploit the situation in all its possible implications and squeeze every ounce of value out of it.

Take a very simple example. If he wanted to describe such a basic operation as ploughing a field, ostensibly to introduce a nostalgic note from the jingling of the harness on the horses, the swish of the soil as it was turned over, and the rich country voice of the ploughman communicating with his team of horses, Geoff would want to know what would happen if the horses took fright and bolted, or if the plough unearthed some sort of treasure, or human bones. He would see this same ploughman and his team taking part in the local ploughing match with all the attendant preparation, the suspense while the competition was in progress, and through the judging right on to the prize winning and the celebrations that followed. All these things would be taken through to their logical conclusions.

He had another faculty that was invaluable – that of analysing the characters that moved across our stage. He knew, and was able to communicate to the listeners, their most intimate thoughts and desires, their hidden fears and hopes, in fact all the built-in tensions and emotions that would emerge when they were involved in a particular situation.

Geoff would not be rushed into taking a decision until he was good and ready. This trait in his make-up was often infuriating when either Ted or I, or both of us, were on to something that we knew was perfect for the programme.

Nine times out of ten he would eventually agree with us, even if it took hours for him to sort things out for himself. Then, having agreed that we were right, he would come up with all sorts of ideas to embellish the story or situation.

Geoff was a countryman through and through. He derived great pleasure from simple, natural things. He would almost lovingly take up a piece of wood and appreciate the natural curves and shape, the pattern of the grain and the texture. He could stand under the cover

101

of a hedge spellbound as he watched nature at work through a stoat performing all its antics as a preliminary to killing a rabbit for food for its young. He would have made a first-class gamekeeper or, perhaps better still, a poacher, not let me hasten to add for any sort of gain, but for the sheer hell and delight of it.

It was an odd turn of fate that the whole of his working life – even when he was in the Forces – should be spent pounding away at a typewriter producing space fiction and millions of words dealing with other forms of extravaganza.

This, then, was the man we had to replace.

It was perhaps fortunate that during the long period of Geoff's failing health the BBC had invited several writers to submit some sample scripts with the thought of having a reserve writer in hand.

One of the contributors to this was John Keir Cross. John had had a long experience in writing for radio and television on a wide range of subjects and forms of presentation, including the first script of *Dr Finlay's Casebook*. He was living on a farm run by his wife in Devon, so he was already possessed of two attributes. He had experience in the writing of serials and was in personal touch with life and work in the countryside.

His sample scripts were sound in construction and carried the right amount of authenticity, well blended with comedy. He had created some good situations and within the limit of a week had brought them to a sound logical conclusion.

It was no easy job for John – or any other writer – to be able to absorb the whole atmosphere of the programme and be able to put the right words and phrases into the mouths of the characters.

As far as the scenes and situations in the overall construction were concerned, this was comparatively easy because they were evolved and developed in joint consultation with Ted and myself, and John was a very experienced writer and was quick to appreciate and act on the slightest lead.

Technically, his scripts were first class, but suddenly to have to take over a whole set of characters that had been created and developed with great care by someone else was no easy task. Our listeners knew and understood the characters as though they were members of their own family, and the slightest deviation in the way they spoke or in their reactions to other characters in the story would, we knew, bring an immediate reaction. So my first job was to spend as much time as possible with John to brief him on the history and background of all the major characters.

It had always been our policy when creating any character that was likely to have a continuing role in the programme to go back well beyond the time that they arrived on the scene. In some cases, it was important to go back for several generations or at least to the time they were born.

Perhaps I should provide an example. Let us take Carol Tregorran – Carol Grey as she was when she arrived on the scene.

She was born as the result of a passionate affair between a young member of the landed aristocracy and an extremely good looking and attractive member of the female staff of the household.

Marriage between these two was impossible and the girl, when the time came when it was no longer possible to hide the fact that she was pregnant, settled for a fairly

103

substantial sum of money paid to her to ensure that she should not make any future claim or contact, and then disappeared to await the birth of the child.

Unfortunately she died in childbirth and the baby Carol was taken into care at a children's home and eventually was fostered out. Then, when she was sixteen, her foster parents died and Carol gravitated to the bright lights of London to get a job.

She had inherited the figure and good looks of her mother and that little bit of something extra from the 'blood' of her father, a very valuable – or dangerous – combination. Add to this the fact that when she was twenty-one the money that had been paid to her mother, and which had been held in trust, was handed over to her in full. This had enabled her to set up her own establishment. I must leave you to fill in your own details of what happened. We all had our own ideas. Let it be sufficient to say that the time came for her to get away into the seclusion of the countryside. It was fortunate that she chose Ambridge and that through her veins coursed the blood of a family that was so closely bound up with 'land', because she experienced a compelling desire to reshape her way of life, and with the remaining capital that she had she bought a small market garden and the greenhouses that had once upon a time been the kitchen gardens of the 'big house'.

The rest of the story you know, and I hope that with this background knowledge you will be able to look back at the way the character of Carol has evolved.

This was what John – or any writer – had to know to allow the continuity of the programme to flow on undisturbed.

He was a very apt pupil, and with his own capacity for

imaginative writing he very soon made a niche for himself in the team.

In many ways John was a complete opposite to Geoff. He was small in stature. He had an impish quality and though he would appear to be self-effacing in his general make-up he was possessed on many occasions with a determination to take a particular course of action that no persuasion or argument could stop.

These qualities all had their effect on the programme, bringing as they did variations in attitude towards any problem that came under discussion.

The biggest problem that we had to face with John as a member of the team was his inherent dislike, almost fear, of the increasing pace of change in the countryside. John loved the past. History fascinated him, and I honestly believe that when he was being shown some new machinery or method in farming practice that was revolutionary, he was genuinely frightened. What he most desired was to wrap himself up in a cocoon woven from his own thoughts of the cosy and nostalgic picture of farming and life in the country that his memory had retained from his youth.

Then John died. He had been a valuable – if not always easy – member of the team and once again we were faced with the problem of finding another writer.

A young man, David Turner, born in humble circumstances in Birmingham, who with guts and determination had worked his way through University to become a teacher, had suddenly emerged as a writer and had hit the headlines through the success of several plays that, while dealing with fairly simple situations, had shown great ability to invest in his characters a tremendous depth of understanding of all aspects of human emotions.

105

This was an essential ingredient of *The Archers*. Did it matter that David had chosen as his subject matter the industrial and urban scene? Could he, with proper briefing, bring this same ability to deal with people in a rural setting? The consensus of opinion was that he would and that he should be invited to prepare some trial scripts.

The same procedure of briefing was carried out, with more emphasis on the pattern of life in rural surroundings. David assimilated the facts very rapidly from this 'cramming' session and the scripts duly arrived. They were not perfect – how could they be in so short a time? – but once again it was agreed that the scripts were full of promise and that, with me available for reference and regular briefings, he would very quickly learn the necessary technique of serial writing and the matter that was important for creating the right environment.

It was quite remarkable how quickly this was achieved. In fact David became so engrossed in the subject that he spent a great deal of time getting out and about in the country to meet the people and soak up the atmosphere. He even went to the extent of acquiring a house in the country where he could go and live while he was writing *The Archers*.

My assessment of David after a long period of working with him was that he was basically an individualist, and although he was quite happy, or so it seemed, working in close collaboration with Ted and myself, as time went on I often had the impression that having to work within the 'strait jacket' of a team was on occasions irksome and inhibiting.

David may not agree with me on this point. He had certainly never expressed any dissatisfaction with the accepted and established formula. But there were occasions when I felt that it must have been very frustrating to him as a creative artist to come up with a story that he personally had conceived, researched and worked out to his own satisfaction, to have it modified or even rejected because it failed to fit in with established principles or character or story continuity.

It must always be remembered that when the editor is going through a script, he must not only be concerned with the accuracy and authenticity of that particular script, but also make a proper assessment of its place in the past, present and future structure of the programme.

No one could have been more willing to basically accept the inevitability of this and David would go to endless trouble to make the necessary rectifications and to see that the modified scripts were delivered on time.

Serial script writing is quite unlike any other form of writing and, with the best will in the world, the number of people who can take the job in their stride, however brilliant they may be in their own field, and become expert is limited because basically it cuts right across the way in which the majority of creative artists like to work things out for themselves.

Time limits have to be strictly observed. There must be a minimum of five scripts in seven days. There are economic limits. The actors one might want to use to carry the story development may not be available. Continuity must at all stages be checked, often right back over a period of years, even in such a detail as the length of a sentence for a character to speak to fit a particular actor's performance.

These are just a few of the handicaps that the writer must accept, and they are not acceptable to all temperaments.

Quite apart from all this, there are occasions in the life of any long-running serial like *The Archers* when, for no obvious reason, an atmosphere of dissension occurs right through the whole organization and this discord in its turn brings fears and doubts into the minds of everyone concerned.

Such a period emerged while David was a member of the team and as a consequence he resigned. There were regrets on both sides when the time came for parting but I am sure that the experience of working together was valuable to both parties.

Once again we had to face the problem of finding a new writer and go through all the business of bringing him fully into the picture. This was not a prospect that any of us fancied, but the problem was quickly solved, right on our own doorstep so to speak.

There was an actor in *The Archers* who had played a leading role right from the start. He even took part in the episodes during the experimental week back in 1949. We had always known him as a writer as well as an actor but had never connected the kind of work he did with the style required for *The Archers*.

Having graduated with first class honours at Birmingham University, he was engaged on research into Anglo-Saxon poetry at Christ Church, Oxford, when he first joined the cast of *The Archers*. During his vacations from Christ Church, he had worked for the Features Department in Birmingham doing research and writing part, if not all, of the resulting documentary programmes. He was a regular contributor to the more serious aspects of children's programmes and was a regular contributor to poetry and other classical programmes. Over the years he had gained a reputation for successful radio adaptations of many of the classics and from time to time produced original plays that fell within the same cultural bracket.

None of us had ever thought of him as a potential writer for *The Archers* and I cannot exactly remember how we discovered that he would be interested in having a trial. But it was arranged and the result was that he was offered the job and has continued to share the writing right up to the present time. His name is Norman Painting, perhaps far better known as Philip Archer. As an Archer script writer he uses a *nom-de-plume* – Bruno Milna.

There was no need for a briefing on the past history of *The Archers*, it was all as familiar to him as it was to us, and under the expert guidance of Ted he very soon acquired the technique of writing in serial form.

Although Norman lived in Birmingham and spent four years at Birmingham University before going on to Oxford, he was now living on a farm in Warwickshire and was naturally closely acquainted with the ways of countryfolk.

Over the years he has set up house on his own in a village near Banbury and plays an active part in the village life, including playing the organ at both the church and the chapel, so he is able to bring a real sense of authenticity into his writing.

From my point of view, Norman has the great ability of taking what may appear to be a dull set of facts and figures, or some important technical document concerning farming, local government or similar material that should be reflected in the programme, and translating it, no, more than that, transforming it into situations that while remaining strictly accurate often fall into the category of comedy.

The team was now complete again and running smoothly, but in order to avoid the kind of problems that had had to be faced in the past with a change-over of writers, it was decided that we should look out for someone who would be willing to act as a reserve, not just waiting for something to happen, but to make a limited number of contributions to the annual output of scripts, and to take part in all the activities that took place behind the scenes in the preparation of the story.

Again, for this Birmingham-based programme we found our answer right on the spot in Birmingham in Brian Hayles – a young man who was already involved in contributing to several successful television serials and knew exactly what it meant to work as part of a team.

For my part, this idea of having a reserve writer is ideal. As a team we and the programme are deriving the benefit of his contribution to discussion, where he brings his active mind, his knowledge and experience of new techniques in the younger medium of television into play.

Throughout this chapter and, in fact, woven into the framework of the whole book, I have brought in the name of Edward J. Mason – Ted to most people – who was in on the programme right from its conception, and remained with it for twenty years. How can one start to evaluate the part he has played and the contribution he has made to the success of *The Archers*?

Millions of words have flowed from his inventive mind on to the paper in his typewriter. As the 'anchor man' he generously gave his practical help and advice to incoming writers, and at every meeting he could be depended upon to find some new twist or angle to a story.

Ted was very much to the fore in all the work that

110

made it possible for *The Archers* to win the *Daily Mail* award on three consecutive occasions as the best radio programme of the year in its category. The same was true when *The Archers* won the Fison Trophy, awarded by the Guild of Agricultural Journalists for the contribution the programme had made to British agriculture and, in 1968, in collaboration with Norman Painting, the Writers' Guild award for the best scripts in their own category.

Need I say more – except that to millions of people the names of *The Archers* and Edward J. Mason are synonymous.

In the last few years of his life, Ted had been a very sick man but his indomitable courage carried him through to the end. His last script was recorded the day before he died. With the passing of Ted, the last link with the origin of *The Archers* was severed. There is no one left in the Corporation who has any personal knowledge of that time when the idea was conceived, or shared the anxieties of the pregnancy, or played a vital part in the birth.

Somehow it brought to me a feeling of great loneliness, like being a stranger at a party where everyone was speaking in a foreign tongue.

IO

The cast

IT is all very well to have a good idea, even a brilliant idea, and to have the ability to get this set down on paper in a dramatic form. But even Shakespeare, Shaw, Noel Coward and all the rest, in the end, had to depend on actors to interpret their work and bring it to life.

We were faced with the same situation in *The Archers*. With very few exceptions we have been extremely fortunate, and this was particularly so in the early years of the programme.

There were two factors, looking back to 1949, that made the task of casting comparatively easy.

Firstly, at that time, the BBC operated on a much more regional basis than they do today, and each of the Regions virtually had complete autonomy when it came to the choice of programme material. Programmes emanating from London were, of course, included in the schedules of any of the Regions, but there was far more material in the daily broadcasts that had a local origin than you would believe possible today.

This had the effect of fostering and encouraging local talent in the cultural and entertainment world, and in order to maintain a high output of programmes there were a considerable number of writers, composers, actors, singers and musicians readily available, and in the case of actors, the fact that they had taken part in a wide variety of programmes from Children's Hour to Revue gave them a versatility that is not easy to find today.

Secondly, the rules and regulations as laid down by Equity today were then almost non-existent and it was possible to use anyone with natural gifts irrespective of whether they had had any previous training or stage and broadcasting experience or held a Union card.

So when it came to the selection of the actors to play the parts of the characters that had been created to bring this 'everyday story of countryfolk' to life, I had a very wide and free choice from among the actors with whom I myself had worked during the time when the major part of my livelihood was derived through radio and who I knew were versatile enough to give the kind of performance that was required.

There was one important decision I had to make. What dialect – if any – should we use? In my own mind, I automatically sited our fictitious village in the West Midlands, but as a Worcestershire man myself I knew that there was no common dialect for the county. Even in districts as close together as Evesham and Pershore there was a very distinct difference in the way the people pronounced words and formed phrases, while at Bromsgrove less than twenty miles away their manner of speech was entirely different. It could easily have been a foreign language to the people of Pershore.

It seemed to me that the only way to tackle the job was to find actors who could portray characters through the tone of their voices but using their own native idiom in the manner in which they accentuated certain words in a sentence. In this way they would be acceptable to listeners in every part of the country.

Looking back on the original cast for the first week of the programme, one finds that they came from Staffordshire, Nottinghamshire, Leicestershire, Warwickshire and Gloucestershire. The one thing that I did not want was a phoney or 'Mummerset' accent. Thank goodness this has never happened.

It is interesting to take a closer look at the people concerned with creating the characters and establishing them so well that millions of listeners took them to their hearts and accepted them as though they were their own friends and acquaintances.

Harry Oakes, who created the part of Dan Archer, was a Staffordshire man from the Potteries. He was a pottery designer, who in the true tradition of the Potteries was keen on music and graduated through the choral society to become a solo singer and as an amateur took part in many musical shows over the years. He had a rich baritone voice and could produce an authentic Staffordshire accent. It was for this ability that he first came into broadcasting to take part in programmes that reflected life in the Potteries.

During the war, when many of the pottery manufacturers had to close down, Harry came to Birmingham to work for the Ministry of Supply. Being on the spot as it were he was easily available for broadcasting and through that wonderful 'nursery', Children's Hour, he enlarged his capacity as an actor and graduated to drama and features.

Harry was a warm and friendly person, with a ready wit, a sense of fun and above all a great sincerity and attention to detail in all he undertook. These natural qualities were just what were wanted for the character of Dan Archer.

Dan Archer had just got to be right. He was the corner stone in the scheme of things. Whatever he said or did, and the kind of actions that he took, the decisions he made and his whole behaviour pattern, had to be accepted by farmers and countrymen, and he had to be recognized as being one of them if we were to get anywhere in our purpose of stimulating progress and greater efficiency in the wide field of farming and the use of land.

In creating the character of Dan, I had gone back in my mind to his great grandfather, a stockman on the Home Farm. He had an acre or two with his cottage and the rights to graze a limited number of animals on the common land.

Over the years, the family had experienced, and had come through, many trials as the fortunes of farming had fluctuated. Slowly their conditions had improved and before our programme started the Archers were tenants of a hundred-acre farm on the estate. Then Dan's father died, leaving a young family with Dan running the farm for his mother. He had come up the hard way and had won through.

The writers had assimilated all this and I firmly believed that it was just as important for the actor to know all that lay behind in the family background in order to get the best out of the words that were given him to say.

Harry Oakes took his briefing well, in spite of the fact that his background was closely associated with industry, but in many ways the fortunes of men and women involved in the pottery industry were very similar to those in farming, and Harry who knew his social history appreciated all that was required of him. It came to him so naturally and he believed in the character so much that when he discarded his city suiting and adopted country tweeds, it all seemed natural and right. So absorbed did he become in his character that he could hold his own in a group of farmers – and look exactly like one of them. He soon became the father figure not only in the programme but with the other members of the cast and spoke and acted on their behalf. It was a very great loss to the programme when he became so ill that he was unable to continue playing the part.

To find a replacement seemed almost impossible but it was essential that the character of Dan Archer should continue.

We auditioned a number of actors without success and then one day when we had almost given up hope a voice came over the loudspeaker in the audition cubicle that might well have been Harry himself. It was Monte Crick.

I had known of Monte for years, not as an actor but as a musical accompanist to the comedian Ronald Frankau, but quite unknown to me he had the great gift of imitation and had quite a repertoire of impersonations of well-known personalities. It was through this ability that he was able to produce an almost authentic Dan Archer voice, and it was not long before he assumed the mantle of the character and the position Harry had held with the rest of the cast.

The same may be said of Edgar Harrison who took

over the part from Monte.

Edgar started his working life in insurance and returned to it after a few years in uniform, but his hobby was acting, and he was well known as an amateur in Bristol and on the professional stage at Weston-super-Mare. For years he had been a regular broadcaster from the West Region, and had played the small part of the cowman at Brookfield in *The Archers*.

It is odd that these three most successful Dans all started their careers in something entirely different from acting.

The character of Doris Archer had to have a country background as authentic as Dan. It was vital that she should have a personality of her own and so provide a picture of a farmer's wife who was capable and could turn her hand to everything in the home and on the farm but at the same time be a mother not only to her own children but to anyone in the village who needed help and comfort.

In my mind, I saw her as the daughter of the head keeper on the estate who, after attending the village school, went into service at the big house where she progressed from kitchen maid to be cook-housekeeper.

She had been courted by Dan for a number of years but would never consider marriage which would mean that she would have to share Brookfield with Dan's mother – she knew that just would not work. So she stayed on with the Lawson-Hopes as a very trusty and respected servant until Dan was left on his own.

Her life at the Manor House, her close contact with the family and her ability to manage the indoor staff provided exactly the right sort of experience to be of value in her new life.

She was very much a part of the era that saw the beginnings of the decline and fall of the old squirearchy through heavy taxation, and was well used to making one pound go as far as two had before, and this was certainly something she would have to do in the early years of her marriage to Dan.

Finding the right actress for this part needed care. She had got to be easily recognizable as a countrywoman but the years spent at the big house would undoubtedly have removed the hard edge of dialect. We needed a voice with plenty of warmth and character in it that one naturally associates with a mother figure. It was very odd that our final choice should fall on a spinster. It was also something of a coincidence that, like Harry Oakes, Gwen Berryman was a singer first.

Gwen was born and brought up in Wolverhampton and music was in her blood. Her father played in the orchestra at the Wesleyan Chapel but Gwen's ambition was to be in opera and she trained at the Birmingham School of Music; very soon she was in the company that was invited to broadcast back in 1926. Her payment at that time was either seven shillings and sixpence or a dinner. Very typically, Gwen, because she enjoys her food, took the dinner. While she was still at the Birmingham School of Music the Opera Society gave a public performance and the *Birmingham Post* music critic at that time picked out Gwen as by far the best actress in the company.

From Birmingham she won a scholarship to the Royal Academy and stayed there for four years during which time she won gold and silver medals and got her L.R.A.M. In her last year at the Academy, she went for an audition at the Lyric, Hammersmith, for the musical play

Derby Day and was selected for the part of Mrs Bones. She went into a film, *Looking on the Bright Side*, with Gracie Fields as the star. Then came a period of ill fortune. Her fiancé, a young doctor, died and Gwen had to give up all thoughts of the theatre because she was ill for quite a considerable period of time, but the call of the theatre and the world of entertainment was still strong. After a period of three years when she was getting occasional engagements as a solo singer and running a baby linen shop in Wolverhampton, she joined the local Repertory Theatre, but once again she was dogged by ill luck and had to leave the Rep. to look after her mother. There was no doubt in my mind when Gwen came for the audition for Doris Archer that she had all the qualities that were required for the part and although she was essentially a town girl, her own personal life had brought her into contact with a very wide range of people and human experience that have since proved to be very valuable in the characterization of Doris Archer.

Gwen still lives in Wolverhampton and to the people of Wolverhampton she is still very much 'our Gwen'.

The three Archer children were already grown up when the programme started. In fact Jack the eldest had been in the Air Force towards the end of the war and had met and married his wife Peggy, a cockney, who was serving in the WAAF on the same station.

Philip had recently finished his year at a Farm Institute and was helping out at Brookfield. Christine had a job with the Borchester Dairies working in the laboratory.

The standard of their education reflected the changes that were taking place in farming. Jack never got past the village school. Philip and Christine both went on to Borchester Grammar School.

119

After the war Jack was very unsettled and, like many a countryman of his age at that time, found it difficult to knuckle down to a steady job. The character was designed to reflect the problems facing young men whose experiences in the Armed Forces had made them become very much aware of wider and more exciting ways of life than working down on the farm.

A wife and growing family was intended to be the steadying influence on Jack but, quite apart from his unsettling experience as a member of the Royal Air Force, he had inherited a certain amount of restlessness from his uncles – Dan's brothers – who had emigrated to Canada and Australia.

Dennis Folwell from Leicester had been a stalwart in the BBC's Midland Repertory Company in addition to being a keen salesman. When he joined the cast of *The Archers* he was pioneering and selling zip fasteners for I.C.I. He had had some professional stage experience in the past and had an active interest in the Leicester Little Theatre. He took to the part of Jack like a duck to water, and I believe he has enjoyed every minute and every experience and situation in which Jack has been involved throughout the whole run of the programme.

The part of Philip was designed to reflect the growing importance of technical education in the future of farming. It was always intended that he should be the 'bright boy' and from the word go it was envisaged that as conditions changed in farming he should take on the mantle of Dan and represent the new generation that would be ready to face the inevitable changes and problems that would emerge on the farming scene.

Norman Painting, alias Bruno Milna, whose background I have already described, seemed an automatic choice, and so it has proved to be.

In the programme, Philip would provide the necessary social and romantic ingredients – this he has done
with two wives and now a growing family. The fact
that Norman was, and still is, a bachelor speaks well
of his abilities to understand and portray a character so
far removed from his own way of life. That is certainly
the way it appears, but who apart from Norman himself
could know his own personal loves and desires?

Christine – in a way like Philip – was created to reflect
the growing opportunities for girls to find a new outlet in
the world of farming and to shake off the shackles of
what seemed to be the inevitable domestic chores either
at home or with friends and relations that was very much
the pattern of the time – the ideal training and experience,
it was thought, to make them in due time good farmers'
wives.

Pamela Mant seemed to me to be tailor-made for the
part. She was young, gay and attractive, and could reflect
and project all this in her voice. She looked right and had
given many excellent performances in plays and programmes in the Midland Region. Added to all this, she
was a very independent young lady who lived in a gypsy
caravan that she kept in a field under the shadow of
Tewkesbury Abbey. She was a horsewoman, too, and was
well able to bring authenticity to the lines and scenes
that reflected the growing interest in horses in the world
of recreation and sport.

June Spencer, who took the part of Peggy, Jack's wife,
was another enthusiastic and capable member of this
Midland-based group of actors and actresses who were
versatile enough to tackle anything.

Nottingham was her home town. Acting was the only

thing she wanted to do. Her very first part was as Mustard-seed in *A Midsummer Night's Dream*. After training she had gained experience as an after-dinner entertainer performing her own comedy material. She has had two books of these sketches and a one-act play published.

When I first knew her she was contributing anything from parts in pantomime to poetry reading and could produce dialects and odd character voices at the drop of a hat. She still can, and many of the odd characters who flit in and out of the programme, from a waitress at a teashop to dear old Mrs Spendlove, are all part of June's comprehensive repertoire. To be a cockney railwayman's daughter was just another part for her to take in her stride and, apart from a short break when she and her husband adopted two children, she has maintained her part throughout the whole run of the programme. We must certainly not forget her portrayal of the naughty Irish girl, Rita Flynn, who led Philip a bit off the straight and narrow.

The family was now complete but a few more characters were needed to get the action moving.

There was Simon, Dan's farmhand, and Walter Gabriel, a wicked but lovable happy-go-lucky neighbour farmer, the sort of person that I hoped the programme would help, and Mr Fairbrother, a really go-ahead businessman who, out of the profits of the war, was enjoying living in the big house and playing at farming.

The farm worker was to be one of the old school and provide some of the comedy. It was important that listeners should laugh with him and enjoy his quips, his jokes and reminiscences.

Among the people who were regular contributors to

broadcasting in Birmingham at that time was Eddie Robinson, the manager of an Employment Exchange in the Black Country, who as an entertainer had built up a wonderful 'Brummagem' working man character, the industrial counterpart of the farm worker. To make the switch from town to country was no trouble to Eddie and he set the pattern that has since been ably followed by Ned Larkin and his son Jethro.

To find an actor to play the part of Walter Gabriel, the granny-reared, muddly old farmer next door, was not so easy, but on the temporary staff of the Midland Region as an announcer at that time was Robert Maudesley who, as a party trick, could produce the most extraordinary vocal effect without any trouble or hurt at all. I'd heard him produce one very gravelly voice with quite a bit of Gloucestershire dialect in it. If only he could modify this a bit it would be ideal. He could and he did.

In an odd sort of way Bob Maudesley was able to switch his own personality on and off at any time. He could be charming and delightful company or he could assume a dry, almost sarcastic attitude with a sharp wit that could hurt if one didn't know the real Bob.

In his own life he had switched from one thing to another and always seemed to make a success of his new-found interest.

He studied medicine at Cambridge where he became interested in drama. With no compunction he dropped medicine and went into films and was making great strides when the war put a stop to everything. He obtained a commission in the Air Force and soon gained promotion with ring after ring being added to his sleeve.

When the war was over, he joined the Overseas News Service of the BBC and from there came to Birmingham as an announcer. The love of acting was still strong and producers were very glad to have him on the spot to take part in the more serious productions.

At this time, Bob and his wife were living in the Cotswolds where they were enjoying and being very successful in buying derelict old cottages and converting them, living in them for a while while the next one was being dealt with and then moving in. One never knew from month to month where the Maudesleys would be living.

Bob was really responsible for establishing Walter Gabriel and building into the part characteristics that many comedians and impressionists of national calibre have used to their own advantage.

The death of Robert Maudesley was a great loss to the programme.

These eight characters laid down the foundations of the programme and set the high standard in the quality and sincerity of performance that has made *The Archers* internationally famous, and perhaps what is almost as important they created the 'family' atmosphere that is still very much in evidence today.

After a short establishment period it was necessary to enlarge the cast and widen the interests of the programme. Very early on the scene was Mr Fairbrother, the wealthy businessman who took over the Manor House and estate vacated by the Lawson-Hopes, the hereditary owners who were forced into selling through heavy taxation.

Leslie Bowman, formerly a Leicester businessman and a member of Leicester Little Theatre, fitted the part like a glove. He had the natural suavity of the character that had been created, but in addition for some inexplicable reason he became fascinated with farm machinery and had set up in a small way as an agricultural contractor and personally enjoyed the work involved in ploughing and cultivating the land.

Philip Archer was taken on to manage the Home Farm for the Fairbrothers and played his cards so cleverly that he married Grace, their only daughter.

Leicester again provided us with another performer, Pauline Saville, to add to the comedy team. She played Peggy's mother, Mrs Perkins, Mrs P. as she is affectionately known by everyone.

Pauline, for a very young lady, had packed in a lot of experience after winning a scholarship to RADA. She had worked in Rep. in Leicester, Manchester and Newcastle-on-Tyne, toured Europe with ENSA and worked at the Vaudeville Theatre in London. Amongst all this, she found time to be involved in charity work as a member of the Junior Business and Professional Women's Club and through her local church.

It always came as a big surprise for visitors to the studios to see an attractive young lady who hardly seemed to be out of her teens playing this crusty and cantankerous old lady.

Although the character of Tom Forrest did not appear in the programme until later, it always seems as though it was there from the beginning. Bob Arnold has played the part throughout its whole run.

Bob was another example of local talent. Born and bred in the Cotswolds, he had been in turn a farm worker, roadman and painter, but above all he was an entertainer doing the round of village concerts, Masonic entertainments and parties – a good rumbustious folk singer. He had broadcast on a number of occasions in programmes with a Cotswold flavour.

The warm friendly 'burr' to his voice was just what was needed to introduce the weekly omnibus edition. This is a mood or scene setter, when he talks to listeners directly about the seasons, the behaviour of the wild life in the woods and fields, or he can reminisce on days and events in his lifetime and regularly recall old sayings and proverbs that have stood the test of time and are still applicable today.

The writing of this introduction each week has been my responsibility. A responsibility, let me add, that provides me with great pleasure.

So proficient did these original characters become that it became more and more difficult to find natural and local people to come into the programme on equal terms, and we had to look more and more to full-time professionals, but there were exceptions, notably when through the deaths of Eddie Robinson and Robert Maudesley it was necessary to find replacements.

In the case of the farm worker it was possible to reshape the programme to make it sound feasible that Simon should pack up work on the farm and his place be taken by a new man, Ned Larkin, but at the same time it was vital that the new character should continue on similar lines and have the same characteristics as his predecessor.

The problem was solved by bringing in Bill Paine. Bill lived in the village of Ebrington a few miles away from Chipping Campden and he had broadcast on a number of occasions when a good Cotswold dialect was essential. Bill was the village plumber and knew all about pumps and wells, and had in his early days worked on the farm. Bill didn't have to act, all he had to do was to be himself and read the lines. There was, however, one very big problem. Bill was a natural comedian and revelled in playing practical jokes. Broadcasting to Bill up to this time had been a bit of fun but there was no time for high spirits and fooling during the rehearsals of *The Archers*. I wrote to Bill and told him that the job was his, but, and I made it clear that it was a big 'but', he would have to assure me that there would be no nonsense in the studio. He assured me that there would be no tricks and except for an occasional lapse all was well. He carried my letter to him in his pocket for years.

Bill had a marvellous face, rosy as a Worcester Pearmain apple, flexible as a soft rubber ball. He could manipulate it into a thousand different shapes and one of his favourite tricks was to stand on the opposite side of the microphone and, with grossly exaggerated facial movement, react to everything that the actor opposite him was trying to put into his part.

It was a shattering experience to try to speak your lines with a face that could move from that of an innocent 'baby' to a 'monster' just two feet away from you.

When Bill died from a heart attack in the train on his way to the studio, it left a very big gap in the programme until we could introduce his imaginary son, Jethro, to carry on the tradition.

Once again, from the memory of the Cotswold plays and programmes that had been a feature in the Midland Region, we were able to find what was wanted. It was George Hart. George was born in Campden almost within view of the village of Ebrington. When he left Campden Grammar School he was apprenticed to gold and silver-smiths in Campden, passed out, and was made a Freeman of the Worshipful Company of Goldsmiths and a Freeman of the City of London.

Like many young sporting countrymen, George was a member of the Territorial Army and saw service in many countries and finished up as a Major. Cricket, football, hockey, motor cycling and hunting were his leisure time interests and he was an active member in local concert parties.

In 1949, George left his trade as a gold and silversmith and went into agricultural engineering. In real life, George is very much a hail fellow well met and enjoys a few pints of cider at his 'local'. There is a lot of George in Jethro Larkin.

The replacement of Robert Maudesley was no easy task. A lot of very well known actors tried hard to reproduce the rasping voice without success. We were almost at the point of despair when someone suggested that we should get Chris Gittins – one of the Regional stalwarts – to have a try.

Chris was a specialist in the local Black Country dialect but was by no means restricted to this kind of work. He had been broadcasting since 1935 in all kinds of programmes right through the war from studios all over the country.

Chris until recently, when he retired, had a partnership in an electrical contracting business but he found time to give twelve years' service as Worcestershire County Organizer for the Baden Powell Scout Guild, command a two-hundred-strong company of Army Cadets and have an active life-long interest as member, committee man and producer of the local operatic society. Today he enjoys the privilege of being either patron or president of these same organizations.

Chris had played a few minor parts in *The Archers* over the years, so that he was not unaware of the task

128

Two typical front pages of the *Borchester Sketch*

The author at work on a script

The author with his wife Betty

that confronted him. As he says himself, 'I was a little undecided about taking on the part to begin with as I was busy with a lot of other contracts and was also suffering from throat trouble which necessitated visits to the hospital and X-rays. I knew it was a difficult part to take over as it required an impersonation of Bob's Walter, Bob's personality and the character of Walter, but I decided to have a go.'

The result of Chris having 'a go' was that he was near enough to get away with it, particularly if he was able to have short appearances over a period of time to make himself familiar with the part and to gain the necessary confidence to let himself go. This was not helped by a national newspaper radio critic tearing him to shreds after his first two minutes' appearance and proceeding to organize a nation-wide opinion poll on whether he should be replaced, by whom, or whether the character should be written out.

The result of the opinion poll was never published, but the very threat urged Chris on to prove that he could do it. He could and did.

Today, rules and regulations virtually prohibit, with very few exceptions, drawing the cast from anywhere except from the ranks of the full professionals. In theory this is, of course, right with so many actors unable to find enough work to keep them fully employed. The professional gives a good polished performance and makes the work of the producer very much easier, but I personally still believe that in a programme like *The Archers* where one is reflecting and presenting ordinary, simple everyday incidents, the performer who has a real life background of a business or professional nature and is meeting ordinary people and facing similar problems in real life can get a truer understanding of the characters they are playing. It is a question that is very arguable but let's look at that character who for many years was the lengthsman round Ambridge and is now the odd job man at the Field Centre – Zebedee Tring – played by Graham Rigby. This is the story of his life in his own words.

'I was in fact a farm lad "betty boy" as it was commonly called in my part of the world, from the age of 16. From washing cow bags I graduated to under cowman/third horseman. Wage in 1943 2s. 6d. per week living in. Learned to plough with horse and tractor, ditch, harrow, etcetera. Went to Agricultural Institute in 1947/48 and got my Agricultural Certificate. On leaving the Institute I became an Assistant Farm Bailiff on the Isle of Man.

'I always had a "bug" for the stage and started by being an impressionist in local W.M. Clubs, also in amateur opera and drama groups. Gave up farming when I found myself driving a horse and cart fast asleep. Farm work and my aspirations didn't fit at all. Turned professional actor in 1950 when I joined Morecambe Repertory Theatre. Attended Northern Theatre School in 1952/55 under Esme Church. Derby Playhouse as Stage Director, leading character actor 1955/60 when I auditioned for *The Archers* and left on the strength of one episode and a promised radio play.

'Whilst "resting" I have been a brickie's labourer, lorry driver, sold Equity Units and double glazing and have also managed a garage. Currently managing a Mortgage Brokers' business.

'Incidentally my conception of Zebedee as a character is built on an old farm worker who did in fact teach me to ditch and hedge. He always wore "yorks", weskitt,

130

soiled flat hat and chow'd baccy with his one remaining
"Pickle Tooth".'

The characters that I have quoted are those by and
large carrying a definite country label or character but it
can also work for what might be determined the straight
parts.

Basil Jones who played the part of John Tregorran was
himself a dealer in antiques.

Ann Cullen who plays Carol was born into a family
with business interests in nursery work and market
gardening.

Apart from the Archer family, the dominating interest
in the parish of Ambridge is the large-scale farmer, Ralph
Bellamy, who has remained a bachelor for a very long
time. Was it a coincidence that a bachelor – Jack
Holloway who lives at an impressive address, Oldswinford
Castle – was selected for the job? I have a sneaky feeling
that there must have been something that brought the
actor and the character on the same wavelength at the
audition, quite apart from the fact that he had previously
played the part of Tony Stobeman, another bachelor.

Jack's personal and business life does not run parallel
with that of Bellamy, but there is much that is recon-
cilable. He was born and brought up in the Black Country
where his parents were in the tough world of business,
had a grammar school education and studied medicine
at Birmingham University. He was commissioned in the
Royal Artillery in 1941 and served in the Western Desert
and went to Italy with the Eighth Indian Division.

After demobilization he joined the family business of
hardware for the building trade. In his spare time he
learnt to be an actor at the Crescent Theatre in Birmingham, worked in television before radio, and became a

part-time news reader for the BBC in Birmingham. Among his other hobbies, he holds a pilot's licence and was Chairman of the General Purposes Committee of a local Flying Club, responsible for organizing the Good-year Air Trophy race, but his first love is the sea. As he says himself, 'Instead of a wife I invested some years ago in a twin-screw ocean-going cruiser, which is equally as expensive, but cannot answer back!'

It is not beyond the realms of possibility that the bachelor reign of Bellamy could come to an end; it would certainly be a coincidence if Jack found himself with a wife instead of a boat. One never knows – on two separate occasions when we decided that Jennifer Archer should become pregnant the actress found herself in the same condition.

I I

'The Archers' and its audience

A RADIO programme like *The Archers* that sets
out to honestly reflect the everyday happenings
in an English country parish is wide open to
all forms of comment and criticism from listeners. In all
my years of association with broadcasting, I cannot
recall any programme that has consistently stimulated
such a heavy volume of correspondence.

I don't mean just fan or critical letters but letters
covering every possible subject ranging from enquiries
about the possibility of a scout troop coming to camp in
one of Dan's fields to the intricacies of Company Law.

Every week, and this has been going on for years, I
personally answer anything up to thirty letters of a technical and critical nature or pleas from charity and other
organizations to include a reference to their particular
interests in the programme. Many of these letters come
from listeners who know the programme so well that they
will actually include a script of a scene covering their

particular interest. Occasionally there will turn up some really vitriolic attack on the way a particular situation has been handled. I often have a strong suspicion that the writer has identified himself or herself with a particular character and takes the situation in which they have become involved as a personal affront.

When Patricia Green joined the cast to eventually marry Philip and become his second wife and mother of his children she came in for a lot of abuse from listeners who had loved the character of Grace, Philip's first wife, and when a photograph of the actress who had played Grace appeared in the *Radio Times* years later, one listener wrote to Patricia and told her in no uncertain terms that she was a bigamist and the children were all bastards.

Very early in the life of the programme we learnt a very valuable lesson about the importance of being accurate. It came from a scene where Carol Grey, as she was then, was bringing her late flowering chrysanthemums into the glasshouse and we wanted to make the point that in order to avoid the plants being attacked by mildew before they had become acclimatized to the new environment the house should be thoroughly cleaned out and sterilized with a sulphur smoke and that the plants should be sprayed with a sulphur-based fungicide. Obviously we had not made it clear that the disinfection of the house by burning sulphur should be done several days before the plants were taken in. The result was that a great many of our listeners got mixed up. They brought their chrysanthemums into the house and then closed all the ventilators and set fire to the sulphur with the result that all their precious plants were killed.

We were very unpopular I can assure you and a

number of listeners wanted to know what we were going to do by way of compensation.

We do try very hard, and often go to endless trouble to ensure that our facts and procedures are accurate but I suppose it is inevitable that with all the goodwill in the world we do make an error or fail to make a technical reference absolutely clear. Then again it is possible for a simple typing error to change the meaning of the fact that was intended.

There is an outstanding example of this that happened many years ago.

Research scientists had discovered and proved beyond all doubt that the addition of up to two hundredweight of nitrogen to the acre spread over a growing cereal crop at a particular stage in its growth would so increase the yield of grain that it was a very profitable thing to do. So, at the right moment Dan would dress his cornfields with two hundredweights of nitrogen to the acre. But for some reason it was not two hundredweights that appeared in the script but two TONS. Somehow or other I failed to notice the error when I was checking the script and as the idea was so new neither the producer nor any member of the cast spotted the mistake and the scene was duly broadcast.

This brought us a flood of correspondence pointing out our error and many of them included cartoon drawings of farmers standing on ladders with a pair of shears in their hands trying to harvest a crop that had shot up towards the sky. Many people were so anxious that they sent us telegrams in the hope that the mistake could be put to rights in the repeat.

One group of farmers who used to meet regularly at the Feathers Hotel at Ledbury sent me the following

135

message by telegram, 'Feathers farmers fear for flattened fields. Two tons, Tut, Tut.'

I knew these farmers well and I racked my brains to send back a suitable reply. At last it came to me and my telegram to them read, 'Flattered Feathers farmers found fault, Typist tipsy, Blameless Baseley.'

I was very unpopular with my secretary.

Much more recently we made another 'boob' and received our due admonitions.

We had been looking for some incident that would go against Gregory Salt, the dairyman at Brookfield, and we decided that if there happened to be a power cut during milking time and Greg had failed to make his routine check on the stand-by engine to run the vacuum pump, Dan Archer could catch him out by leaving the milking clusters on the cows while he fiddled about with the stand-by engine trying to get it to work. Yes, we were pleased with this, but in developing the story we forgot one simple point. That if the vacuum pump stopped the milking clusters would not remain on the cows but would fall off and lie on the floor and would need to be sterilized before they could be replaced.

This would have made an equally good story but, alas, we had overlooked this very simple basic fact, but not the listeners, and for weeks I received scores of letters pointing out the error. There was a curious thing about this correspondence, most of it came from farmers' wives. I couldn't help wondering if the farmers got their wives to write rather than admit that they listened to the programme themselves to keep up to date with any new developments in farming that we always try to reflect.

Trouble does not always come from mistakes. It can come if we move on to deal with likely changes in the farming scene. There is one quite outstanding example of this.

When the programme started Dan had a herd of dairy shorthorn cows. This was quite right and natural because this breed of cattle was the most numerous throughout the whole of the British Isles, but a few years after our programme got under way there came a challenge from Friesian cattle. This breed that was mainly imported from Holland was noted for producing a very high yield of milk – and although at that time there were doubts about the butterfat content it was a great temptation to a growing number of farmers to change breeds to get a greater bulk of milk from an equal number of cattle. I wanted Dan Archer to be among those who were changing over.

We had a very good relationship with the Shorthorn Society and I thought it would be common courtesy to let the Secretary know what was in my mind.

Naturally he was disappointed that we were likely to take such an action and duly reported the matter to his Council. The Council were very well aware of the influence the programme was having in the farming world and they could well imagine that if an increasing number of farmers followed the lead given by Dan Archer, this could to some degree jeopardize the livelihood of their members, particularly those who were producing pedigree stock.

Someone on the Council had doubts as to whether within the terms of its charter the BBC could be a party to anything that could jeopardize the livelihood of a section of the community.

The legal representatives of the Society and the BBC got together on the matter. Apparently there was some truth in the Society's assumption and it was finally agreed between the parties that we should not proceed with this aspect of our story for a fixed period of years.

I was naturally very disappointed not to be topical on such an important happening in the world of farming. As a dairy farmer, I wanted Dan to keep up with the times and I felt that if he remained a dairy farmer with short-horns over the period of time covered by the restriction he could well lose the image of a forward-looking farmer that we had been so careful to build up.

The only way out of this that I could see was for Dan to change his pattern of farming and go over to beef production until such time as he could go back to milk production using Friesians.

So we planned that there should be an outbreak of foot and mouth disease in the district and that all Dan's stock would have to be destroyed.

This provided us with some highly dramatic material and incidentally allowed us to get some valuable information across to farmers and the general public.

Once the all clear had been given for restocking, Dan went into beef production, but always longing to be back on milk which, of course, he did at the appropriate time. Today Friesians are the major source of milk in this country.

Another interesting example of the influence the programme can have on listeners came from a very simple and short reference to the fact that a small piece of rock or lump sulphur added to a dog's drinking water could be beneficial to the health of the dog. So great was the rush on chemists for rock sulphur that the whole of the country's stock held by retail outlets was swallowed up within a few days.

Our references to this kind of thing stimulated a private company to start an Archer Monitoring Service, so that information could be passed on to the manufacturers or distributors concerned. Whether this still exists today I do not know but quite recently when one of our old country characters was talking about the menace of rats he trotted out a recipe for an effective and fairly safe poison that contained glycerine. Almost by the very next post I received a letter from a Public Relations organization saying, 'We shall be very grateful to receive any information on the episode in *The Archers* concerned with killing rats, including the original formula, which you are able to give us. I am writing on behalf of the United Kingdom Glycerine Producers' Association.'

I was happy to let the writer have the recipe which was as follows: —

Pinhead Oatmeal	80%
Castor Sugar	10%
Glycerine	5%
Warfarin	5%

In the district in which I live, cowslips grow everywhere and are classified as weeds particularly when they invade our gardens. The making of cowslip wine is a very normal procedure, but when in the introduction to the Sunday omnibus edition of *The Archers*, Tom Forrest quoted a recipe that he always used for making this particular wine, we were very severely 'ticked off' by several listeners who were also keen botanists for stimulating the destruction of this plant. Yorkshire listeners were to the forefront in this issue, as apparently the cowslip has quite disappeared in that county.

In the early days of the programme, Geoffrey Webb, in his anxiety to create a homely atmosphere on a number of occasions, credited Doris Archer as something of an expert in making 'apple crumble'. The number of enquiries for the recipe was so great that the only way we could think of to satisfy the demand was to write a scene in which Doris explained to a visitor just exactly how she made her 'apple crumble'. It took quite some time to get hold of anyone who could tell us how to make it – because none of us knew – but eventually we managed it, and the scene was duly written and broadcast.

This was a great mistake, because far from satisfying listeners' demands it only stimulated still more listeners to write for the recipe. Even today, some twenty years later, we still get an occasional request for a list of ingredients and the method of making and cooking. So, just to be on the safe side, here it is.

Apple Crumble (or Cracknel)
    1 lb. cooking apples
    $\frac{1}{2} - \frac{3}{4}$ lb. self raising flour with a little sugar added
      to the flour
    2 – 4 ozs. margarine (not lard)
    sugar to taste

Boil the apples until they are soft enough to mash up, in a small quantity of water – just enough to stop them burning. Add the sugar according to taste. Then put the flour in a bowl – not forgetting the touch of sugar added to the flour – and cut in the margarine. Rub well together until the mixture is crumbly.

Now pour the mashed apple into a greased pie dish and sprinkle the crumbly flour and margarine mixture over the apples so as to cover them completely. Then put it in a moderate oven and bake it till it is a nice brown on top.

It has always been very flattering to know that listeners

take the contents of the programme quite seriously, but it can on occasions be slightly embarrassing. Let me give you an example.

At one period in the programme, Dan Archer was having difficulty in finding the right sort of cowman. Imagine my surprise when in the post one morning was a letter from a student at the Harper Adams Agricultural College in Shropshire, applying for the job.

At first, of course, I thought it was a joke, but the young man had gone to great pains with the letter, stating why he thought he had the right qualifications for the job, so after reading it again very carefully I had to take it as a serious application.

I knew the Principal of the College, Bill Price, very well so I rang him up to ask him if there was a student at the College of the same name as my correspondent. Yes, there was. Was he the sort of student who would play practical jokes? No, he was a very serious student. Then I told him about the letter, in fact I read it over to him in confidence. What did he think, was it a joke or was it serious?

'Oh I think it is quite genuine,' said Bill. 'You see, this young man had got himself fixed up with a job to go to at the end of term and then unfortunately the farmer died and the farm and all the stock is to be sold and my student is left high and dry with only a few weeks to go till he leaves college.'

I wrote as kind a letter as I could and hoped that he would find a job as good as the one with Dan Archer had appeared to be.

Another letter, much more recent this time, came from a listener at Oxted in Surrey who wrote, 'We have been faithful followers of *The Archers* for some years now and

141

are interested in their activities. Some three months ago, I bought the October edition of the *Borchester Echo* and in it there are pictures of Trigger, Doris Archer's Jack Russell. He appears to have the same build and markings as our little bitch and I am wondering if it would be at all possible to have him as a mate for our Tinka. Would you be able to let me have the name of the owner or kennels?'

Trigger happens to be my own dog, so I did get in touch with Tinka's owners to say that I was sure Trigger would oblige (and in due course the mating took place).

There is another event concerning Ambridge animals that is worth recounting as an illustration of the belief that listeners have in regard to the authenticity of the programme.

Many years ago, Christine Archer was to ride in the Ladies' Race at the Ambridge Hunt Point-to-Point and this was causing a lot of excitement in the village and odds were being laid about the horse in the Bull. But it did come as a surprise to me when a real live 'bookie' rang me up to say that he had a number of clients who wanted to make a bet on the result of the race, so could I let him know how we proposed to deal with it.

He had the idea that we would be broadcasting from a real race on the day and that ours was a real live genuine horse and obviously did not want to turn any money away if that was the case. When I told him that the episode that included the race had already been recorded and that at least a hundred people knew the result, he knew exactly what to do.

In the early days of the programme we used to receive a vast amount of correspondence from members of Women's Institutes who thought that we strayed from the rules in the way that we reflected their organization, and, in particular, the record we used for the singing of *Jerusalem* came in for a lot of critical comment as not representing the way it was sung. Some writers complained that it was too good, others that it was not good enough. Actually it was a record made by a group of professional singers.

To get over this problem I thought the only way to deal with it was to make a recording at a W.I. Meeting. My wife was at that time a member of the committee of her Institute and I asked her if she thought this would be possible. She consulted the President who agreed, but suggested that it had better be recorded without the knowledge of the members, and then to tell them after it was finished.

With great secrecy the recording engineer planted the microphone and drove his vehicle round the back of the hall out of sight.

The members duly arrived and the meeting started in the usual way with the singing of *Jerusalem*. There were one or possibly two notes on the piano that stuck a bit but this was fairly normal in any village hall.

Before the meeting proper started the President informed the members of what had happened, and the record was played back to them. They were delighted – fame at last had come to Finstall W.I.

For our part we could hardly wait to use the record in the programme to show that we did take notice of listeners' letters and were willing to take steps to right our wrongs. Then it happened – dozens of letters came from Women's Institutes all over the country letting us know in no uncertain terms that no W.I. could possibly sing as badly as this and that we ought to be ashamed of ourselves.

There was another occasion when we needed a special recording of music, this time of the Borchester Silver Band playing at the Ambridge fête. The only recordings which were available were by the top bands – and besides this we wanted the band to march through the village on its way to the fête.

It so happened that at that time I was President of my own local town band and I asked them if they would do this for me. They were delighted, and it was arranged that it should be recorded early one Sunday morning in a quiet road by the cattle market.

At the appointed time the band arrived resplendent in their uniforms and it was obvious that some spit and polish had been applied to the instruments.

It was a bitterly cold morning but they lined up and started their march with the man on the big drum being quite determined that he should be heard. Within a few seconds the noise had attracted the attention of a dog who barked and howled his way along with them and nothing we could do would stop him.

For our purpose the recording was perfect but not very flattering to the band. I am no musician but I am led to understand that the cold weather was responsible for quite a variation in pitch among the instruments.

This record is one of the treasures in the Archers archives.

The actors in the programme are in great demand to open fêtes and bazaars, and make personal appearances at all kinds of functions all over the country. Gwen Berryman tells me that she has travelled thousands of miles and now knows her way around Britain without ever having to look at a map. She has some amusing stories to tell.

At Pontefract her housekeeper went with her for company and amused herself by going round the various side shows including 'Bowling for a Pig'. At the end of the day she was more than a bit surprised to learn that she had the highest score and had won the pig. It certainly came as a shock to Gwen when she tried to work out how on earth she was going to take a live pig in the back of her car all the way to Wolverhampton – and what she could do with it when she got there. There was a happy ending – they gave her the money instead.

It was at this same function that Gwen was presented with a four-pound box of Pontefract cakes. Knowing full well that she could not possibly eat them all herself she took them along to the studio to share with the rest of the cast. Harry Oakes took one look at the box and said, 'Didn't they give you a toilet roll to go with them?'

Gwen had another embarrassing moment at Peterborough. Six of the members of the cast had gone as official guests of the Mayor to a big town function. Their day started with a civic reception at 11 a.m. but as there was a long wait till lunch, accompanied by the Mayor they were taken along to the principal hotel to meet some of the local celebrities and have a drink. While they were sat around in a circle Gwen spotted a waiter with something carefully covered over with a napkin taking a good look at the assembled company. Then he advanced on Gwen with everyone watching, and said, 'Excuse me, Madam, would this be yours?' He carefully lifted the corner of the napkin and there on the silver salver was one false tooth on a gold wire. In his careful study of the company, the waiter had noticed a gap between Gwen's two central top teeth and assumed that this was where

145

the false tooth should really be. The incident nearly spoilt Gwen's day, but all was well, the tooth belonged to Dennis Folwell – it was a new acquisition and he was not quite used to it, so rather than face lunch with it in he had surreptitiously removed it and placed it in his outside breast pocket and when he pulled out his handkerchief – out came the tooth on the floor where the waiter found it.

At another function – this time at Newmarket – a great fan of *The Archers* drove over from Downham Market to meet Gwen. At the end of their chat he asked her if she liked strawberries – of course she did – thinking he wanted to present her with a small basket. Imagine her surprise when later in the day her admirer turned up with twelve chips of strawberries and twelve pots of cream to go with them. He stacked them in the back of her car and hoped that the rest of the cast would enjoy them. It wasn't until he had gone and Gwen was on her way home that she realized that as it was a holiday week-end there were no rehearsals for a week and the ripening fruit had to be used. It was years before Gwen could face a strawberry again.

Leslie Bowman had gone to open a village fête and a farm wagon was drawn into position to make a platform. Leslie, immaculately turned out as usual, climbed up the steps to address the assembled company. As he warmed to his subject he stepped back to give emphasis to a point and stepped on to a rotting plank which immediately gave way and Leslie disappeared as though through a trap door, just leaving his head on view.

Something of a similar nature happened to Chris Gittins at Caerphilly, where once again the platform party were using a large hay wagon. Chris was the last one to get up on the wagon and just as he was about to take his seat, someone moved it. Chris did a backward somersault into the crowd – this got the biggest laugh of the day, as no doubt everyone thought that this was all part of the Walter Gabriel act.

The character of Walter Gabriel has always been one of love or hate to listeners, but in spite of the odd and often crazy things that he does in the programme I am sure that he is loved by the majority. One thing is certain, that is that Chris makes him sound so real that when he makes a personal appearance in public he is expected to do all the things that he is supposed to do in the programme.

There was a time when Walter Gabriel made some handbags to sell to a Borchester store. All went well till he ran out of curtain rings that he had used for handles, and what happened? Within a few days Chris started receiving parcels of rings of all sorts and sizes, large wooden ones, small ones, steel, bakelite and brass rings. Before long he had received so many that his garden shed was full of them and when he opened the door they rolled down the path.

Curtain rings are not the only items to be sent to Walter. He has received new socks, bundles of hay, turnips, and even parcels of bluebottle flies at a time when the character was considering starting a maggot farm.

Chris has been expected to drive steam traction engines, he's made a balloon ascent, taken part in clay pigeon shoots, been challenged at skittles and shown his hand at ploughing with horses.

It is, of course, extremely gratifying to know that *The Archers* can make such an impact on listeners, that they believe it all to be true. This belief has been very much

147

in evidence throughout the whole run of the programme.

When Grace died, flowers arrived at the studios for the funeral. When some of the characters have been due to have a baby, parcels of beautiful baby clothes have arrived. Parents have written to me for advice on opportunities for their sons in agriculture.

Dan Archer has received genuine orders for turkeys at Christmas time and at one period, when Dan was going through something of a financial crisis, a small boy arrived at the commissionaire's desk at the entrance to the studios in Broad Street, Birmingham, with the contents of his money box which he had brought to help Dan out of his troubles.

There is a much more serious side to this belief in the programme. Questions in the House have found us a place in Hansard. The *Farmer and Stockbreeder* has written a serious article on the Archer method of farming. I.C.I. have made a study of the pattern of cropping and stocking and general management and put their findings through the computer, which came up with some first-class information on how we could reorganize the pattern and procedure to make the whole enterprise more profitable. This valuable piece of documentation has been a big influence on the thinking for the future of the farming that forms the basis of the programme.

Through the success of *The Archers* I have on several occasions spoken at conferences organized by the Food and Agriculture Organization and the Organization for European Economic Co-operation on using the techniques that have been employed in the programme as a means of agricultural education in those areas of the world that find it difficult to understand modern techniques through the normal methods of education.

We have been very flattered to be invited by such an august body as the Royal Agricultural Society to be their guests at the Royal Show, and many of the big commercial concerns involved with farm machinery and equipment, feeding stuffs and chemicals have welcomed me to their research establishments and experimental farms so that I can keep abreast of the times.

The Archers, throughout its long run, has always been a source of good 'copy' for the Press on their news as well as their feature pages. There was a time when for months the *Daily Sketch* produced a weekly supplement entirely devoted to *The Archers* – the *Borchester Sketch*, a development from the BBC's own publication, the *Borchester Echo*.

The requests to use the name of *The Archers* for advertising purposes has had to be severely controlled but it was inevitable that a few loopholes should be found, not only commercially but by charity promotions.

The biggest fiddle of all for a good cause was done by a parson friend of mine.

In order to get an authentic atmosphere I had asked my parson friend if we could use his church to record the wedding scene when Philip and Grace were married. We had already recorded and used the peal of bells and the organ on several occasions.

Permission was granted, the date was fixed, and everything was lined up, including a fee to cover the expenses of bell ringers and organist and for the facility of being able to have the use of the church.

The roof of the church badly needed some repairs, and the money was to be used for this purpose. A very enterprising chap was my parson friend, and with the smell of money in his nostrils he had the idea that if he could get

149

a congregation in to watch the recording being made he could take up a collection and so add to the fund. So he leaked the information to the local Press, who in turn passed the information on to the nationals with the result that when the actors tried to get to the church the roads were blocked with cars and coaches and every square inch of the church was occupied.

How Tony Shryane managed to get a successful recording among such chaos I do not know, but he did. What is more, work was able to start on the roof repairs.

My friend has long since left the parish, but the association of *The Archers* and the village of Hanbury is still carried on in spite of the fact that Ambridge and Hanbury have no connection from a farming or social point of view, except that the photograph we use to represent Brookfield farmhouse is the home of my wife's sister and is located right on the edge of the parish.

When television became established in this country a great many people wanted to know if *The Archers* could come even more to life through this new medium.

It would be possible, but only at very great expense, and with a complete reorganization of technique. But for my part I am sure it would be a mistake because over the years listeners have built up their own mental image of the characters and of the village in which they live and work. It would be inevitable that this image would be shattered in one way or another and cause more disappointment than pleasure.

There was evidence enough of this when a play that was specially written by Geoffrey Webb and Edward Mason for presentation on the stage failed. Not because there was anything wrong with the play, or the actors who took part, but everyone who went to see the play

had their own very fixed ideas on how the characters
should look, how they should be dressed, what their
various mannerisms should be, even the settings in which
they moved – and of course there was bound to be disappointment. No, radio is the ideal medium for the
programme.

I sometimes wonder now that I have the value of hind-
sight if all the mystique that is so much a part of the
programme wouldn't have held up longer and stronger
for far more people if there had been less exposure by
way of photographs, personal appearances, Press and all
the other forms of so-called 'promotion' that go on in
the world today. It's just a thought, perhaps I am wrong,
it could well be that personal contact with the people
intimately concerned in the project, and the appreciation
of the sincerity of everyone concerned with all the various
aspects of the programme, have played their part in
cementing the fellowship that so obviously exists between
us and the public.

1 2

A typical day at Brookfield Farm

＊＊＊＊＊＊＊＊＊＊＊＊＊＊＊＊＊＊＊＊＊＊＊＊＊＊

IN the twenty-one years in which *The Archers* has been so much a part of my life, there have been revolutionary changes in farming and the pattern of village life that even the most fanciful could never have believed possible in such a short time.

It seems unbelievable that when we started the programme the combine harvester was still a novelty in this country. 'Oh, it might work in Canada and America but not in the weather we get here unless it's a very dry time.' This was the considered opinion of many of the experts and was reflected down the line to the majority of the individual farmers.

Horses on farms outnumbered tractors by six to one. When we first met Dan Archer, all the motive power on his farm was supplied by two Shire horses.

I find it fascinating to go back through the first few scripts and discover what a comparatively simple and uncluttered life they led at Brookfield Farm. I find it

very hard to believe that these scripts at that time truth-
fully reflected life on the majority of farms in the West
Midlands. But they did.

Let me recall a typical day.

Soon after five o'clock, Dan would wake and strike a
match to light the candle by the side of his bed to look at
his pocket watch to check the time. He'd pull on his socks
and trousers which were conveniently hung on the brass
knob of the iron bedstead – more than likely he would
have slept in his shirt and long pants – he'd take the
candle and go downstairs, light the fire in the range, fill
the kettle from the pump over the stone sink, and suspend
it over the stick fire by means of a hook or a chain. Then,
while the kettle boiled, he'd make his way down the
garden to the earth closet screened by an ancient yew
tree. By the light of the hurricane lantern he would read
bits from the local newspaper before he tore a piece off
to crumple up in his hand to soften it to use as toilet
paper.

Back to the kitchen where the kettle would have boiled,
he'd make a pot of tea, add some wood blocks to the fire,
pull on and lace up his boots, grab his brown smock from
behind the door, then, carrying his lantern in his hand,
make his way across the yard to the cowshed.

The cows would already be in their places munching
hay from the racks in front of them and Simon, the farm
worker, who had brought the cows in with him on the
way from his cottage to the farm, would be squeezing
between the cows to get to the 'boosey' or manger to give
them a feed of chopped mangels, chaff, kibbled beans
and broken up oil cake.

It would probably take them the best part of two hours
to milk the thirty cows by hand into open buckets, cool

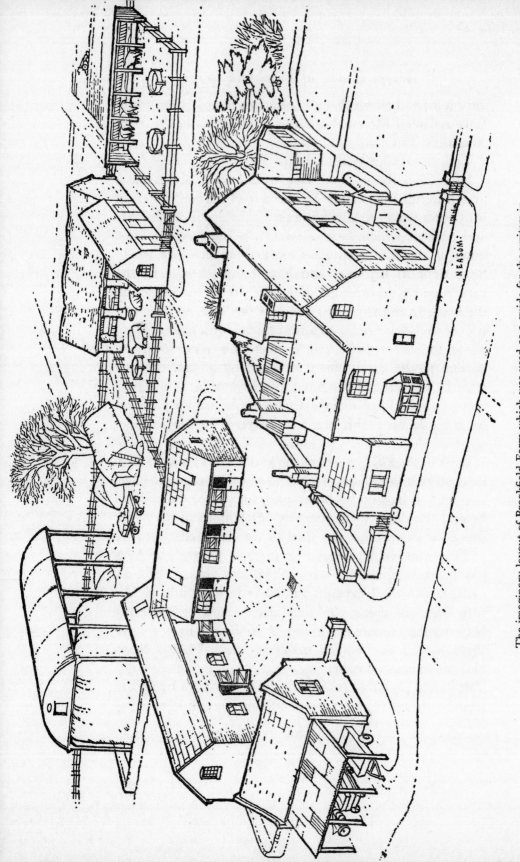

The imaginary layout of Brookfield Farm which was used as a guide for the writers in the early days

the milk and get it into the churns. Then, while Dan returned to the house to write the labels that were to be attached to the churns, Simon would harness the pony, put him into the milk float, and load up the churns ready to be rushed to the local station to catch the milk train.

While Dan was on his way to the station, Simon would return the cows to the field and bring the working horses back with him and give them a feed of kibbled beans, crushed oats and chaff. Then he'd go back to his cottage for breakfast – more than likely cold boiled fat bacon from his own pig.

By this time Doris would be up and about, put breakfast on to cook, and while she was waiting for Dan, go out and scatter Indian corn or wheat in the rickyard for her hens.

After breakfast there would be the job of feeding the calves and the pigs – the pigs were kept in sties and fed on a sloppy mixture of 'Sharps' or barley meal to finish them off. They were well and truly fat pigs.

In the cowshed the manure had to be removed and stacked in a heap in the yard – what a task it was to try to get the cobbled floor of the shed washed and brushed down clean. Food for the following day was ground, chopped and mixed, hay and straw carried in on a fork to fill up the racks or spread out as bedding.

If it was market day, the horse and float came into use again to carry sheep or pigs, but cattle had to walk.

At haymaking time, Simon would be out cutting the mowing grass with his pair horse mower at the first light of day while the dew was on the grass and the work on 'making' and carting the hay would continue until the late evening and the return of the dew, not forgetting that at four o'clock the slow procession of cows made

155

their way to their own individual standings in the cowshed for the afternoon milking when they would swish their tails and shake their heads to try to rid themselves of troublesome flies.

Ploughing was done by the pair horse single furrow plough, potatoes 'set' by hand, manure carted from the yard and dragged out of the tipping carts into heaps to be spread later by hand.

Ricks of hay were built in the fields where they would be fed to the stock, the corn was stored in stacks to be threshed out later when the travelling steam threshing tackle would visit the farms in turn and extra labour would be hired to deal with the rush of extra work.

The boys from the village would turn up with stout sticks in their hands and a mixture of breeds of dogs at their heels to deal with the rats that had made their homes in the ricks.

Labour was still comparatively cheap – minimum wage just under five pounds a week. There were 800,000 workers on the land in 1950 – today it is just over 300,000.

Practically all the farmers were tenants on the Lawson-Hope estate, and tradesmen and craftsmen, like the blacksmith, the wheelwright, the carpenter, the mason and the miller, were still part of the pattern of village life.

There was no electricity in the village or on the farm. Wood and oil were the main sources of heat and light. Water was pumped or drawn up from wells as it had been for generations, till suddenly some well-meaning health inspector came along to take a sample and declare it unfit for human consumption – but I suspect the well was condemned to force the villagers to contribute to the cost of a piped water supply that was demanded by a few fanatics.

156

A typical day at Brookfield Farm

Motor cars were still very much of a luxury for the majority of countryfolk. Tar macadam was just being used to surface the lanes by two men with special brushes fed by a flexible tube from the rear of a horse-drawn 'tar pot'.

The village was still a leisurely place where one could lean against the doorpost at the blacksmith's and watch that magical event when the blacksmith tucked the hoof of a great animal between his legs and the slit in his leather apron and applied the red hot shoe to the horny surface to bed it in so that it would be a snug fit after it was nailed on. This was a magical moment for everyone, old and young alike, as the clouds of smoke enveloped the smith and billowed out of the open doorway.

It was still the time when one would expect to see the roadman sitting in his upturned wheelbarrow eating his breakfast, a slice of bacon that he had cooked on his shovel over a wood fire, laid on a thick slice of bread that had been wiped in the fat. It was a 'thumbit' and with his sharp pocket knife he would slice off a portion and convey it on the point of the blade into his mouth.

You could expect to see a genuine horse-drawn gypsy caravan pulled up on a wide grass verge with all the family involved in making pegs which they hoped to sell in the village so that they could buy their essential bread and meat and groceries.

The policeman still walked his beat, and woe betide those gypsies if their 'lurcher' dogs had provided ingredients for the pot, simmering over the fire, that could in any way be classified as 'game'.

What a contrast with today. Just twenty-one years later. Electricity – probably the most important development – is now in every house and on every farm even in

157

the most remote areas. Virtually every farm operation is mechanized and in many cases automated. Livestock is fed on scientifically balanced food, weeds and pests are controlled by chemical means, animal health is rapidly acquiring a level almost equivalent to that of human beings.

Motorways and modern transport, particularly the motor-car, have made villages accessible and attractive to an ever-increasing number of urban dwellers. Greater affluence among the population as a whole has made it possible to transform the simplest country cottage into a desirable residence with all 'mod. cons'. Villages and towns have become interdependent – the towns for labour, the villages for the facilities not available in the towns.

Education has played its part and the present generation no longer stay at the village school for the whole of their education but have opportunities, and take them, far beyond those available to their parents, and they are equal to anyone, no matter to what social class they may belong.

Where do we go from here? What are the changes that *The Archers* will reflect in the future in the social life of the village, the work on the farms, the human problems, that emerge in any era?

One thing is quite certain: progress will not stop or slow down. I believe that we shall see an acceleration in the pace of change as farming, the background of rural life, becomes even more industrialized than it is today.

By the end of the present decade I expect to see most of our food production in the hands of no more than 100,000 farmers operating on large scale units or in groups, integrated with or financially backed by industry or finance corporations intimately concerned in food processing and the production of the ever-increasing demand for convenience foods.

I expect most of the land in the South-West of England, Wales and huge areas north of Derbyshire to be designated as areas for leisure and recreation, where animals will be used as mowing machines during the spring and summer and return to either over-winter in fully automated intensive housing or to abattoirs to be processed for human consumption.

I see most of our milk being produced at low cost from grass during the spring and summer and processed into a form from which it can be reconstituted. All potatoes will be either canned, frozen or dried, and this same process will be still further developed throughout the whole range of vegetables.

Those farmers who, like the small shopkeepers and industrialists, will have to give way under the economic strain of these developments, will find other occupations in the towns or from the tourist trade or, for some, act as wardens in leisure, sports and recreational areas.

If, as could well happen, atomic energy is made freely available for peaceful purposes, then many of the hazards associated with weather and farming in this country could be overcome.

What of the villages? It is here that I see the greatest changes. Any village within forty or fifty miles of an urban or industrial area will, through its easy access by motorway, become a dormitory for commuters. It will take far more than a decade for the new pattern of population to become unified in the way village life has been in the past through intermarriage and hereditary ownership of land and property. A new social structure will need to be built, more modern facilities demanded

159

and a real effort made on everyone's part to preserve the natural environment and amenities. Without this our villages could soon become extensions of suburbia and lose the charm that makes our villages and countryside the envy of the world.

This is the task that must be tackled in a programme like *The Archers* – to reflect and bring to life all the human, administrative and economic problems as they emerge. The programme may well have to sacrifice some of its nostalgia, but wherever there are people there will be a good story to tell.

Twenty-one years ago, the programme was specifically designed to help farmers, their workers and everyone associated with agriculture and country life in any capacity, to keep in step with the times. The future holds a new challenge – to address itself to the population as a whole and help them to get the best from the use of the countryside and to enjoy all the pleasures and facilities that we who have lived in the country for most of our lives have accepted as our right and privilege.